Carmela's Cucina

also by Carmela Hobbins

**Celebrations
with
Carmela's Cucina**

Carmela's Cucina

by

Carmela Tursi Hobbins

NODIN PRESS

Designed and edited by John Toren

Cover photograph Jerry Stebbins
Cover food styled by Susan Lukens

Interior photographs by Kathryn Short and Dr. Bart Muldowney
Photo p 116, Arlene Gardinier

Nodin Press, LLC
530 N. Third Street,
Suite 120
Minneapolis, MN
55401

This book is in memory of my beloved grandmothers, Carmela Pigneri Tursi and Anna Basta Fazio. It is dedicated to my mother, Sarah Fazio Tursi, who taught me from a very early age the importance of family and good food. These three women could take the simplest foods and create something for all to treasure.

Thank you for helping me to preserve our Italian heritage.

table of contents

Acknowledgements

Grazie mille to my wonderful parents, Joe and Sarah Tursi, for their patience and encouragement during the writing of this book, for providing me with so much family history, and for handing down generations of family recipes.

Bravo to my brother, Bobby, and sister-in-law, Amy, for maintaining a family treasure, the Latin King Restaurant, and for sharing their love of Italian food with the Des Moines, Iowa community and with our family and many friends.

Special thanks to my aunt Darlene Torri Tursi, my uncle Paul, and to their family, for providing recipes from my aunt's family in Northern Italy and for being a constant source of support throughout this book.

Thanks to my *cara cugini*, Peter Tursi, and his family; and to Lenny (Dale) Tursi, Loretta Tursi Sieman, and her mother, Mary Severino Tursi, for providing recipes and stories from their families.

Grazie tanto to my Italian tutor Daniela Ruggiero for offering her specialty recipes, for translating recipe titles for me, and for sharing her love of authentic southern Italian food.

Warmest thanks to a group of wonderful women, my college friends, Marla Kauzlarich Borer, Martha Gearty, Lynn Matte Gibbs, Michelle Manatt, and Christina Pietro Sheran for helping me with recipe development, photography, and being the best long time friends anyone could ask for.

Grazie mille to my friend Bart Muldowney for the fabulous photos that he recorded of our culinary week in Tuscany. To Norma Lattan Muldowney and her sister Alyce Lattan Caspers for sharing their Italian heritage with me.

Cent' anni to Anna Maria Vellutini and Lido Martini for introducing us to the unique pleasures of Tuscan cuisine through their cooking classes on our culinary tours of Italy, and to my dear friends Doug Haynes and Doris Fortino, whose gracious hospitality and effort provide us with a wonderful experience of Italy through her food, wine, and culture.

Many, many thanks to my dear friend Kathryn Short for taking endless photographs of the food pictured throughout this book. The many hours of her hard work and effort have made my recipes look exceptional.

To Diedre Shapani, thanks for spending so much time consulting and directing me through this process.

Much appreciation to Norton Stillman, my publisher at Nodin Press, John Toren, my very creative editor, food stylist Susan Lukens, and photographer Jerry Stebbins, for the vision they had for *Carmela's Cucina* and for making my dream a reality.

Con tuto il mio amore to the four men in my life. To Brian, whose retelling of family stories have helped to document our family history. His creative ability is extraordinary; he can make one laugh and cry at the same time. To Patrick, for always making me keep my sense of humor no matter how discouraged I became, for giving me the confidence to continue, and for assisting me in my classes. To Teddy, for always being available to taste test the recipes and food that I prepared during the writing of this book and for giving me much inspiration for recipe development. Finally, to Bob, my wonderful husband—without him I would have abandoned this project. Thank you for being with me every step of the way, editing, critiquing and praising my work, for allowing me to dream and then for giving me the freedom to make my dreams come true.

introduction

This is a book about Italian food—how to prepare it, how to enjoy it, how to share it. But where I come from, food is inseparable from family. This is why my story must begin with the immigration of my grandparents, Frank and Carmela Pigneri Tursi, along with their son, Joseph Tursi (later to become my father), to the United States from Terravecchia, a hill town in Calabria, in southern Italy. My paternal grandfather had actually emigrated to America to start a new life in 1921, just before my father was born. It would be another nine years before my father and grandmother were able to join him. Just before their departure, however, my father became ill and was unable to complete the journey with his mother. Six months later he followed her, accompanied by his grandmother, Nonna Maria.

Meanwhile, my maternal grandfather,

Frank, Peter, and Paul Tursi

Giuseppe Fazio, from the small Calabrian town of Scala Coeli, was making his way to New York City to join his older brother. Eventually, he too found himself in Des Moines, where he met my grandmother, Anna Basta, from Cosenza in Calabria. The two married when my grandmother was fifteen years old.

Both families ended up living on Loomis Avenue on the south side of Des Moines. While Grandpa Tursi worked on the railroad, Grandpa Fazio worked as a mason. Grandma Fazio and her parents operated the neighborhood grocery store, while Grandma Tursi tended to her home. My father's first job was as a shoe repairman, which led to a very long career in the clothing business. In 1950 my father married my mother, Sarah Fazio, at St. Anthony's Catholic Church.

I was born in 1951, and my parents and I lived for several years in the apartment above my grandparents' home. A year later my brother Frank was born. (My two younger brothers, Joe and Bobby, were born many years later.) With one set of grandparents living just below us and the other set of grandparents just down the street, Frank and I were able to spend a great deal of time with them. Our great grandmothers also looked after us. With my father trying to build his business and my mother going to school and helping my father on the weekends, much of our childcare was left to our grandmothers and great grandmothers.

My mother, Sarah Fazio Tursi

And that is where my love of cooking all began—on the laps of my grandmothers. Under their guidance we spent a good deal of time tending to the vegetables in the garden, going to the market for special ingredients, and cooking. The shared goal was to have good food waiting when my grandfathers and parents arrived home from work. This was what "home" was about.

I can still clearly see my grandmothers baking bread and making their own homemade pastas. "Store bought" would not do for them. In the summer their large gardens produced enough fruits and vegetables for the year's use. There were apple, pear, peach and cherry trees to provide fresh fruit not only for the table, but for pies and cakes, too. There were tomatoes, peppers, onions, beans, eggplant and fresh herbs enough for side dishes, sauces and condiments. I can recall the rows of jars filled with vegetables and sauces neatly lined up on their cellar shelves to last the year. My parents and grandparents were determined to duplicate in their new home what they had left behind in Italy. They even had grape vines and made their own wine which they stored in large oak barrels in the cellar.

Always at my grandmothers' side, I would pat the dough that they had made, stir the sauces that were simmering on the stove, and help wash the vegetables that would eventually fill mason jars in their cellars and pantries. But most of all, I loved to eat the foods that we prepared. We would spread the breads, fresh from the hot oven, with butter and devour them; we would dip the pita frittas in sugar and consume them eagerly; and we savored the pasta sauces made with our own home-grown tomatoes and basil. So bountiful were their vegetable gardens, in fact, that in the summer Frank and I would set up a little table on the corner and sell tomatoes for 25 cents a pound. This was my first job, and I loved stacking the tomatoes carefully and watching for customers to make a purchase on their way home from work. Grandma Tursi in her thrifty way would dole out 50 cents to us for our week's labor— just enough for an ice cream cone at Reed's Ice Cream just around the corner, where Frank and I were regulars. The remaining profits were put into our bank accounts.

After the blur of time that was high school and college, I found myself married and starting a household of my own in Minneapolis, Minnesota. At this point, I came to realize that the Italian culture and food I had taken so much for granted in Des Moines, with its large Italian American community, were not necessarily to be found everywhere. I began to explore the cuisines of other areas, hosting small dinner parties to provide opportunities for experimentation. Julia Child became my television mentor, and I immersed myself in preparing elaborate menus for 4 to 5 couples for a Saturday evening dinner party that would occupy my free moments for days. As trying as it could be to find the time to do this, I discovered that I enjoyed the preparation and the company; both served as a pleasant diversion from the responsibilities of being a young wife and parent.

In 1983 my long-time friend Marla Kauzlarich Borer suggested that we begin our own catering business, since we both loved to cook and entertain. Thus began the five-year run of a successful catering business, "Occasions Inc." Our specialty was catering to those hosts who were too busy to do what we loved doing—cocktail parties, small weddings and dinner parties. We worked hand in hand for five years, but the demands of her three young daughters and my three young sons ultimately dictated that we reluctantly close the business.

For years after that, I devoted my time to raising a family, keeping a home, teaching part-time at our local elementary school, and volunteering. Throughout all this I continued to hone my culinary skills by entertaining often and hosting larger and more elaborate parties. As our children grew and became more independent, I was able to do more traveling, and I visited Italy frequently to attend cooking schools. In 2003 I decided it was time for me to make use of my teaching skills to begin teaching the cuisine of Italy. I have applied my love of all things Italian to Carmela's Cucina, a series of small private cooking classes that I offer regularly. I also teach in many of the Twin Cities' area cooking schools.

My grandparents never returned to Italy; when they left their homes, that chapter in their lives was closed. Instead, they focused on the future and made wonderful homes for their families in the United States. The occasional letter or small package from Calabria would arrive, containing the spices that my grandmothers used in their baking. They would send small gifts to the brothers and sisters who had remained behind, never to be seen again. I, on the other hand, have been blessed to travel to Italy frequently. With the help of good friends in Tuscany, Doris Fortino and her husband Doug Haynes, we host culinary tours of Tuscany and Liguria from our "headquarters" in the beautiful villa, Il Mulino di Torrigiani, just outside of Lucca. As we enjoy the beauty of the place, learn the classic recipes and techniques, dine in the best of restaurants, visit the wineries, markets and shops, and bask in the warmth of the wonderful Italian people, I cannot help but thank those who introduced me to the joys of this way of life so many years ago.

Guests, friends and family have frequently asked me for my Italian recipes, many of which go back three generations. A few years ago I decided it was time to preserve this part of my heritage for my own children and nieces and nephews. And so this book, *Carmela's Cucina*, has evolved. In it you will find tried and true recipes that have been passed down among family and friends for years. You will also find recipes from my culinary tours in Tuscany and from my brother Bobby's Latin King Restaurant in Des Moines, Iowa. It is my hope that you will try many of these recipes and make them your family favorites as well. My grandparents are gone now, but the traditions and simple joys that they brought with them from the old country live on through the food and recipes that they passed on to us.

It is our custom to begin our meal with a toast, so let me welcome you properly to my cucina: Salute! Buon appetito!

Antipasti

For my family, a holiday or a Sunday meant dinner with "i nonni," the grandparents. My grandfather would begin the meal by going to each of the children's places and dropping a tiny splash of his homemade wine into our glasses of bubbly 7-Up, turning the drink a lovely pink. The 7-Up could not be too cold—just slightly cool. "We do not want to hurt your stomach," he would say each time he preformed the ritual. Then would come the antipasti that my grandmother had prepared—small bits of cheese, cured meats, roasted peppers, tomatoes, olives, and breads.

My grandfather ate slowly, always the last to finish his meal. We children would grow bored, leaving the table to play long before the adults rose from their places.

As I grew older, I began to ask about my grandfather's seeming fascination with the stomach. Nothing too cold or too hot could be consumed; it would hurt the stomach. You must eat and chew slowly to aid the digestion. Do not eat large portions; eat several small ones instead. Always, always enjoy several glasses of wine with a meal. This was the way it was done at their table. My non-Italian friends did not eat this way. They would sit down to plates heaped at once with meatloaf, mashed potatoes and gravy, vegetables and bread. We, on the other hand, ate our meals in a series of small courses.

Much later I learned that most native Italians begin their meal with an aperitif— vermouth with soda or a small glass of wine—along with their antipasti. This aids in "opening the stomach" (which apparently has been closed) to accommodate the food about to be consumed.

After the antipasti, a pasta course or primo piatto, is served—something light and not too large—followed by a secondo piatto of meat with vegetables or salad, known as contorni. Each of the courses is to be savored in an unhurried atmosphere interspersed with lively conversation. Some cheese, fruit, and nuts would follow, with a sweet dessert wine and coffee or espresso. Only on special occasions were desserts or "dolci" served.

And then, just when you are convinced it is not possible to consume one more thing, the small glasses with the digestivos appear. My grandfather's favorite was anisette, the strong, clear licorice flavored liqueur. It was far too potent for young children to drink. Today, to assist in the digestion of a meal such as this, I prefer to sip on an icy limoncello or a small glass of vin santo.

My grandparents must have had it right; they all lived into their late eighties before they passed away, with the exception of my maternal grandmother who left us just a few years ago at the age of ninety-three. And even during our visits in her final year, she always offered us a little anisette to sip along with her.

The antipasti I share with you in this book can be just the beginning of such a meal or, if several are made together, may serve as a meal themselves. Today antipasti parties are quite popular, and around Italy there are Spuntino bars serving a complete menu of "tutto antipasto," featuring a vast array of antipasti continually served in courses. However you choose to serve these small tidbits, I hope that you are enjoying them with many friends and family. And so we begin this chapter as my grandfather began his meals, with a toast to his family, to your health. Salute!

Mixed Antipasti

antipasto misto

All meals in Italy begin with a little antipasto of meats and cheeses. What I have done with this *antipasto misto* is to take all of the typical ingredients and mix them together to create a wonderful beginning to a meal.

> 1 9-oz. jar of green olives with pimento
> 1 6-oz. jar of marinated artichoke hearts
> 1 6-oz. can of tuna
> 1 4-oz. can black olives
> 1 4-oz. can mushrooms
> 1 2-oz. can anchovies (optional)
> 8 oz. of provolone cheese
> 6-8 oz. salami
> thinly sliced bread

Marinade for antipasto misto

> 1 cup olive oil
> ¼ teaspoon pepper
> ½ teaspoon salt
> ¼ cup red wine vinegar
> 1 teaspoon Italian seasoning blend

Drain olives and chop roughly. Drain the remaining ingredients. Cut the cheese and salami into thin strips. Add to the drained mixture. In a large bowl, pour the marinade over all and toss well. Marinate overnight in the refrigerator. Stir occasionally.

When ready to serve, pour into a beautiful lettuce-lined bowl. Top with a sprig of parsley and serve with thinly-sliced bread or crackers.

This makes a wonderful sandwich. Just split a focaccia and spread with the antipasto mixture. This sandwich could also be heated in the oven and served warm.

MAKES 12 SERVINGS

Artichoke Squares

quadratini di carciofi

Cut these into small squares, insert a frilled toothpick, and serve on a white platter.

> 2 6-oz. jars marinated artichoke hearts
> 1 small onion, finely chopped
> 4 eggs
> ¼ cup fine, dry bread crumbs
> ⅛ teaspoon pepper
> ⅛ teaspoon oregano
> ¼ teaspoon salt
> 2 cups grated mozzarella cheese
> 2 tablespoons chopped fresh parsley

Drain artichokes, saving the marinade from the jar. Sauté onion in marinade. Cut up artichokes. Beat eggs, add crumbs and seasoning. Stir in the mozzarella cheese and parsley. Turn into a 7x11 inch greased pan. Bake at 325° for 30 minutes. Let cool a bit before cutting.

These squares can be served warm or at room temperature. Provolone can be substituted for mozzarella.

MAKES 12 SERVINGS

Making crostini the old-fashioned way

Crostini

Crostini are delicious with a piece of cheese, a few olives, a salad, or as a base for many antipasti.

1 baguette
⅓ cup olive oil
one garlic clove

Cut baguette into ¼-inch slices. Brush each slice of bread with olive oil and place on a cookie sheet. Bake in a 350° degree oven for 7-8 munutes. Turn crostini and bake for an additional 7-8 minutes.

When cool enough to handle, rub with the garlic clove. Cool and store in an air-tight container for up to 5 days, or freeze for up to 1 month.

MAKES 24 SERVINGS

Mozzarella Crostini

crostini con mozzarella

1 cup shredded mozzarella cheese
8 oz. sun-dried tomatoes in olive oil, drained
1 baguette

Chop tomatoes. Combine with mozzarella cheese and spoon 2-3 teaspoons on crostini. Bake in a pre-heated 400° oven for about 5 minutes, or until cheese melts.

MAKES 24 SERVINGS

Crab Crostini

crostini con polpa granchio

To decorate, add a small sprig of parsley and a tiny segment of lemon just before serving.

⅓ cup Parmesan cheese
¾ cup mayonnaise
¼ cup chopped onion
dash Worcestershire sauce
dash of salt and pepper
1 6½-oz. can crab meat, drained
1 baguette
butter

Slice baguette, butter bottom of each slice, and place on cookie sheet. Blend ingedients and spread on top of bread slices. Broil until golden brown and puffed, checking frequently to make sure topping doesn't burn.

MAKES 36 SERVINGS

Shrimp Crostini

crostini di gamberi

¼ cup chopped onion
1 5-oz. can shrimp
1 3-oz. package cream cheese
1 cup mayonnaise
1 teaspoon lemon juice
salt, pepper, and dill weed to taste
¼ cup Parmesan cheese
1 baguette
soft butter
pimento and parsley for garnish

Chop onion finely in a food processor. Add can of drained shrimp and pulse a few times. Cut cream cheese into small cubes, and add, along with mayonnaise, lemon juice, salt, pepper, dill weed and Parmesan cheese. Pulse until it makes a spreadable paste.

Cut baguette thinly and butter bottom side of each slice. Spread shrimp mixture thinly on top. Garnish with a small pieces of pimento and parsley. Bake at 350° for 10 minutes, or until lightly browned. Yields about 36.

These toasts can be assembled and frozen until ready to use. If frozen, remove from freezer and let thaw for 30 minutes, then bake according to directions.

MAKES 36 SERVINGS

Crostini with Pears, Gorgonzola, and Honey

crostini con pere, gorgonzola e miele

My good friend Christina Pietro Sheran shared this recipe with me. She comes from a large Italian family similar to mine. Our friendship goes back 35 years, to the time when she, her husband John, my husband Bob, and I were all students at Creighton University in Omaha. Their children are friends with our children, and our families often have dinner together.

Christina served this dish one year during the holidays and we all proclaimed it *delizioso*.

> 6 thick slices country-style bread
> 1 large ripe firm pear
> 5½ oz. gorgonzola dolce (sweet)
> 3 tablespoons brown sugar
> 1 tablespoon butter
> 4 teaspoons honey
> freshly ground black pepper

Toast bread slices briefly in a heated oven.

Peel the pear and cut in half vertically. Core and cut each half into eight thin slices. Melt the sugar and butter in a sauté pan and add the pear slices. Cook on medium heat until pear slices begin to caramelize lightly and soften. There should be a bit of syrupy liquid with the pears. A few drops of water can be added if there is not sufficient liquid.

Divide gorgonzola and spread over toasted bread. Return bread to oven; melt gorgonzola. Place pears on bread and drizzle with honey. Sprinkle with freshly-ground black pepper.

MAKES 6 SERVINGS

Artichoke Crostini

crostini di carciofi

Enjoy with a glass of chilled white wine.

> 1 baguette
> ⅓ cup olive oil
> 1 14-oz. can artichoke hearts
> 1 cup mayonaise
> 1 cup grated Parmesan cheese
> 4 oz. grated mozzarella cheese
> ½ teaspoon garlic, minced

Cut the baguette into ¼-inch slices. Brush both sides of bread with olive oil. Toast in a 400° oven for about 5 minutes on each side, or until golden brown. Meanwhile, combine other ingredients. Mix well. Spoon 2-3 teaspoons onto each crostini. Return to a 400° oven and bake until cheese melts.

The spread for this easy and delicious antipasto can be prepared ahead and kept refrigerated for up to a week.

MAKES 36 SERVINGS

Grazietta's Chicken Liver Crostini

crostini con fegatini di pollo

Grazietta is the owner of La Querica, a cooking school in the Chianti region of Italy. She was my first teacher in Italy, and everything that came out of her kitchen was both easy to prepare and wonderful to eat. The first thing she taught me was to use only fresh ingredients.

olive oil
½ large onion, chopped
1 lb. chicken livers
½ cup red wine
2 teaspoons capers
salt, pepper
1 teaspoon butter

Cover bottom of pan with olive oil. Sauté chopped onions, then add livers and wine. Cook for about 20 minutes, until cooked through. Add capers and process in food processor until smooth. Add a pinch of salt, pepper, and 1 teaspoon butter. Pulse one more time.

Serve warm or cold on crostini or crackers.

MAKES 12 SERVINGS

Italian Party Pizzas

pizzette alla napoletana

The Neapolitans invented pizza, but people everywhere love it. My version is quite small, which is why I call them pizzette.

1 lb. Italian sweet sausage
1 lb. lean hamburger
1 lb. shredded mozzarella cheese
1 teaspoon basil
1 teaspoon oregano
¼ teaspoon garlic powder
1-2 teaspoons chopped parsley
1 cup your favorite pasta sauce
1 baguette, sliced on the diagonal
butter, softened

Brown sausage and hamburger together, drain well. Add the cheese, basil, oregano, garlic powder, salt, pepper, and sauce to the meat and mix well. Cut bread thinly on the diagonal. Butter the bottom of each slice and arrange on a cookie sheet. Top with meat and cheese mixture, and bake at 350° for about 10 minutes or until bubbly and hot.

These can be made ahead and stored in the freezer for up to 3 months.

MAKES 36 SERVINGS

Milanese Appetizer Cups

tartine di proscuitto e ricotta

These antipasto cups can be made ahead and re-heated. They can be served hot, cold, or at room temperature. They are simple to make and sure to please any crowd.

1 10-oz. package chopped spinach
8 oz. carton ricotta
½ cup grated Parmesan cheese
1 cup chopped mushrooms
2 tablespoons minced onion
¼ teaspoon dried oregano
¼ teaspoon salt
1 egg, beaten
24 thin slices proscuitto, about 2 inches square
dairy sour cream
2 green onions, thinly sliced

Preheat oven to 350°. Cook spinach according to package directions, and drain well. Combine spinach, ricotta, Parmesan, mushrooms, onion, oregano, salt, and egg.

   Butter 24 mini-muffin cups. Press a slice of proscuitto into each cup. Spoon mixture on top. Bake for 20-25 minutes, or until a knife inserted in the muffin comes out clean. Remove from oven and let stand for 5 minutes. Arrange on a tray and garnish with sour cream and onion.

MAKES 24 SERVINGS

Mini Quiche

tortine di uova

During the period when my long-time friend Marla Kuazlarich Borer and I owned Occasions Catering, this was one of our most-requested items. They're easy to make and quite delicious. Try other fillings, such as prosciutto, spinach and mushroom, or crab.

1 package butter-flake dinner rolls
1 4½-oz. can shrimp, drained
1 beaten egg
½ cup light cream
½ teaspoon salt
dash of pepper
1⅓ oz. Swiss cheese

Preheat oven to 375°. Grease 24 mini-quiche tins. Divide each dinner roll in half by separating the layers, and press into a tin. Place 1 shrimp in each shell. Combine eggs, cream, salt, and pepper. Divide cream mixture evenly among shells using about 2 teaspoons for each shell. Slice the cheese and place a small piece on top of each quiche. Bake for about 20 minutes or until golden brown.

These quiches can be frozen on a cookie sheet, then stored in a plastic container for up to three months. To serve, thaw and reheat at 375° for 10-12 minutes. Bacon or ham could be substituted for the shrimp.

MAKES 24 SERVINGS

Rolled Egg Omelet

frittata arrotolata

This is wonderful served for breakfast or lunch. It can also be made as an antipasto course. Serve with focaccia and proscuitto.

**1 package frozen chopped spinach, thawed,
   drained, and squeezed dry, or
   1¼ lb. fresh spinach, washed, and
   stems removed
3 tablespoons olive oil
½ cup chopped onion
1 8-oz. package mushrooms, chopped fine
½ cup grated Parmesan cheese
⅓ cup pine nuts
12 large eggs
Salt and pepper**

Preheat oven to 350°. In a frying pan over low heat, warm 2 tablespoons of olive oil. Add onion and sauté about 1 minute; add mushrooms and sauté about 5 minutes. Add the spinach and sauté another 3 to 5 minutes, breaking up the spinach. Add salt and pepper. When cooled slightly add pine nuts and cheese.

In a bowl beat the eggs with salt and pepper to taste. Line a jellyroll pan with foil and spray with Pam. Pour egg mixture into pan and bake for 15 to 20 minutes or until the eggs are set.

Pick up foil and slide it onto a clean kitchen towel. Spread the spinach mixture over it evenly, leaving a 1-inch border. Roll up the omelet lengthwise to enclose the filling completely. Place seam-side down in an oven-proof dish and heat through—about 10 minutes. Cut into slices, and serve warm or at room temperature.

MAKES 8 SERVINGS

Calzone

calazone ripieno

This is a favorite of our family for lunch or a snack. Try other fillings, too.

**1 package frozen dinner roll dough
pepperoni slices
6 oz. sliced mozzarella cheese
5 cups of your favorite spaghetti or pesto sauce**

Thaw bread dough according to package directions, but while it is still very cold stretch each piece into a flat round. Top the dough with two slices of pepperoni and a slice of mozzarella. Fold over in half to form a turn-over, and seal edges tightly to prevent the cheese from seeping out. (At this point the calzone can be frozen on a cookie sheet to be used later.)

Bake in a 350° oven for 15-20 minutes or until they are golden brown.

To serve, put a container of the sauce for dipping on a platter or basket, and surround it with the calzone.

MAKES 24 SERVINGS

Prosciutto-wrapped Asparagus Spears

asparagi con prosciutto crudo

I like to serve this antipasto as part of a brunch, instead of ham or bacon. When we are at the lake, I will often make a platter to take out on the pontoon during our late afternoon cruise.

12 asparagus spears
12 basil leaves
12 sliced prosciutto
herbed goat-cheese or flavored cream cheese
¾ cup olive oil
¼ cup balsamic vinegar
salt and pepper

Blanch asparagus in boiling water for 3 minutes. Drain and plunge asparagus into an ice-water bath. Let the asparagus sit in the ice bath for 10 minutes. Remove and dry with paper towels.

Place a slice of prosciutto on a cutting board. Lay a basil leaf on top. Add a dab of cheese on the end of the prosciutto to help seal the rolls. Set asparagus spear on top and roll to close.

Repeat with the remaining asparagus, prosciutto, and basil. Cover and refrigerate.

Before serving cut each roll in half. Drizzle with a mixture of olive oil and balsamic vinegar, to which a pinch of salt and pepper has been added.

MAKES 6 SERVINGS

Bruschetta with Spinach and Mushrooms

bruschetta spinaci e funghi

I created this antipasto one year using leftover stuffing from our Easter leg of lamb.

1 small package chopped frozen spinach
4 tablespoons olive oil
1 cup chopped onion
3 or 4 garlic cloves, minced
1 8-oz. package mushrooms, chopped
½ cup mayonnaise
1 cup grated Parmesan cheese
1 thinly sliced baguette
butter

Thaw spinach and drain well. Heat 4 tablespoons olive oil in a pan, add onions and garlic and sauté until transparent. Add chopped mushrooms and sauté. When the mushrooms are cooked through add spinach and cook until heated. Remove from heat and cool. Add mayonnaise and grated cheese. Mix to combine all the ingredients.

Butter bottom of each slice of bread, spread mixture on top, and arrange slices on a cookie sheet. Bake at 350° for 10 minutes, or until hot and bubbly.

These can be assembled and frozen for up to three months. To bake, thaw for about 15 minutes and bake at 350° until hot and bubbly.

MAKES 36 SERVINGS

Steak Bruschetta

bruschetta alla fiorentina

This is a delicious and colorful antipasto to make in the summer, when basil is plentiful and the tomatoes are at their peak.

1 cup tomatoes, seeded and diced
2 tablespoons chopped fresh basil
1 tablespoon finely chopped onion
1 tablespoon olive oil
1 teaspoon balsamic vinegar
1 clove garlic, minced
1-2 lb. bottom round steak
1 loaf Italian bread
salt
bunch of arugula

Combine tomatoes, basil, onion, olive oil, and vinegar, and set aside.

Place steak on heated grill and cook for 7 minutes, turning once for medium doneness. Let rest for 5 minutes. Slice meat across the grain into ¼ inch slices.

Slice bread in half lengthwise. Brush bread with olive oil and grill until golden brown on cut side. Sprinkle bread with salt and pepper. Place greens and steak on bread, and garnish with tomato mixture.

To make for an appetizer, slice bread into ½-inch slices, then grill, and arrange greens, steak, and tomato mixture on top.

MAKES 12 SERVINGS

Mushroom Bruschetta

bruschetta di funghi

The Italians love to hunt mushrooms. I remember as a young girl going out with my father and his friend to forage for them. After gathering a basketful we would head for home. That's when my mother's work began. She would clean the mushrooms with a damp towel and then sauté them in oil. She would add just a little crushed red pepper and serve them on toasted Italian bread.

Today in Italy you will still see people out hunting the elusive fungi. Like my father, they know which mushrooms are safe to eat and which are not. If you're unsure about such things, then rely on store-bought varieties to satisfy your needs.

½ lb. mushrooms
bread slices
6 garlic cloves
olive oil
salt and pepper
½ cup Parmesan cheese, shaved thin

Trim and clean mushrooms. Cut bread into slices. Preheat oven to 350°.

In a small baking dish, toss 5 of the garlic cloves with 1 teaspoon olive oil. Roast for 30 minutes, turning occasionally, until easily pierced with a knife.

Cut mushrooms into ¼-inch slices. Set aside.

In a large skillet, heat 1 teaspoon olive oil over medium-high heat. Mince the remaining clove of garlic and sauté until it begins to soften. Do not let it brown. Add mushrooms and cook, stirring occasionally, until the mushrooms are soft and their liquid has evaporated. Season with salt and pepper.

Bake bread slices until golden brown, about 12 minutes. Remove from oven and set aside.

Peel and mash the roasted garlic. Place it in a bowl with 1 tablespoon plus 1 teaspoon olive oil. Mash until smooth. Spread mashed garlic over bread slices and place on serving plates. Top with the mushrooms, sprinkle with the cheese, and serve.

MAKES 12 SERVINGS

Tortellini on Skewers

spiedini di tortellini

2-3 packages tortellini
skewers
spaghetti or pesto sauce

Cook tortellini according to package directions. Cool in water. Thread 3 tortellini on the end of a skewer. Arrange skewers on a platter like spokes, with a bowl of sauce in the center. Garnish with parsley.

MAKES 24 SERVINGS

Mushroom Paté

paté di funghi

This velvety-smooth paté is excellent on crostini. I suggest that you use crimini mushrooms or a mix of crimini and button mushrooms for a very flavorable spread.

½ lb. fresh mushrooms
2 tablespoons unsalted butter
1 tablespoon dry sherry
4 oz. cream cheese
4 oz. herb-flavored Alouette or Boursin cheese

Wash, dry, and chop mushrooms; then sauté in butter and sherry for 5-10 minutes or until tender and

almost all of the liquid from the mushrooms has evaporated. Place in a food processor or blender with cheeses and mix thoroughly. Refrigerate, covered, for at least 3 hours before serving, preferably overnight. Serve on crackers or crostini.

This paté will keep well for about 10 days in a tight-fitting container, though it doesn't freeze well.

MAKES 1½ CUPS

Ricotta Cheese Ball

palline di ricotta e formaggio

At Il Mulino, the villa that hosts our tours, the cheeseman drives up in his car with fresh ricotta weekly. Doug buys a pound of the creamy cheese that Doris will make into her *Torta di Ricotta*. Back in the States our ricotta will be purchased at the supermarket, in all likelihood. But whether you're spreading it on toast or making this delicious cheese ball, always purchase the highest quality ricotta you can find.

1 lb. ricotta cheese
½ lb. cheddar cheese, shredded
2 oz. jack cheese with jalapeno
     peppers, shredded
2 cloves garlic, minced
1 tablespoon green onion, minced
2 teaspoons Worcestershire sauce
½ teaspoon salt
dash black pepper
1 teaspoon lemon juice
¼ teaspoon ground cumin
½ teaspoon chopped walnuts

Combine cheeses in a food processor. Process until smooth. Add garlic, onion, Worcestershire sauce, salt, pepper, lemon juice, and cumin. Blend well. Shape into a ball and sprinkle with walnuts.

Serve with vegetables or crackers.

MAKES 12 SERVINGS

The weekly delivery of fresh ricotta

Ricotta Pie

torta di ricotta

Year after year, Doris Fortino and Doug Haynes have this torta on the table waiting for us upon our arrival at Il Mulino, following our long journey from the States. With a mixed green salad, some crusty bread, and a glass of sparkling Prosecco wine, we are revitalized, and ready to begin our culinary week.

For the crust:

> 1¼ cups unbleached all-purpose flour
> ½ teaspoon salt
> 7 tablespoons cold unsalted butter
> 3 tablespoons ice water
> unsalted butter for greasing the tart pan

For the filling:

> 1 lb. fresh ricotta (best quality you can find)
> ½ cup good quality Parmesan cheese
> ½ cup aged Pecorino-Romano cheese
> 2 heaping tablespoons basil pesto (can be
>   found in the dairy case with other
>   refrigerated sauces)
> 1 large egg
> generous dash of salt and white pepper

For the topping:

> 3-4 good quality vine-ripened tomatoes-sliced
>   thin, less than ¼ inch, if possible
> 3 tablespoons olive oil
> 3-4 basil leaves, chopped
> Greek or Italian pitted olives (optional)

Preheat oven to 350°.

To make the crust, in a mixing bowl mix flour and salt together. Add butter. Using 2 knives, cut into the butter until it forms into pea-shapes. Sprinkle cold water over the mixture and keep working it with the 2 knives. Then, using your hands, gather up dough mixture (without overworking the dough) and form into a little ball. Place in a bowl and chill for 30 minutes and up to 2 hours.

On a lightly-floured board, quickly roll out the dough into a circle large enough to fit in a 9-inch pan with a 2-inch overlap around the edges. Place dough into the tart pan, fold over the edges, and press and pinch along sides of pan.

In a mixing bowl, add ricotta, Parmesan, Pecorino, pesto, salt, and white pepper. Mix together. Then add egg and mix thoroughly.

Fill the pastry shell with the mixture. Arrange tomatoes over the filling, sprinkle chopped basil leaves over the top, and drizzle olive oil over the tomatoes to moisten. Bake until crust is golden and filling has puffed up. At that point you can be certain that the filling is cooked through (about 30-40 minutes).

Serve warm or at room temperature.

Greek or Italian pitted olives can also be added to the filling before baking. Premade refrigerated crusts could be substituted for the homemade version.

MAKES 8 SERVINGS

During my childhood and adolescence the family Christmas celebration invariably included a Christmas Eve meal with the traditional Seven Fishes. As a child I did not like this tradition at all. "Who would serve seven fishes for a holiday?" I always asked. In those days, December 24 was a day of fasting and abstinence—no meat. While my non-Catholic friends were dining on turkey, ham, and rib roasts, I was doomed to seven fishes.

As I got older I began to question my grandmothers and my mother about the tradition. Why seven? Which fish need to be included? What does this tradition have to do with the birth of Baby Jesus? But no one could give me an answer. They just replied that their mothers before them made the seven fishes and the tradition must carry on. And so it did.

Today we do not have all seven fishes, but we always have some fish—usually a shrimp cocktail that we all devour before my mother has even finished cooking the *baccala* (salt cod fish) and the stuffed calamari that she has been slaving over all day. The Church has relaxed its rules—we are now permitted to eat meat—so there is always beef, and of course it would not be a holiday in our family unless there was some manicotti, ravioli, or a stuffed pasta on the menu.

Why Seven Fishes? I still don't have the answer. Some say for the seven days of the week, others for the seven sacraments of the Catholic Church or even the seven gifts of the Holy Spirit. But I've grown to like the idea because it is a tradition. So on Christmas Eve, I will make a Seafood Antipasti for my family to enjoy. There won't be all seven fishes, but in some small way I am still connecting my family to their Italian roots. And for me that is the most important thing anyway.

Seafood Antipasto

antipasto di fruitti di mare

This antipasto is not only a wonderful primi course, but could stand alone as a light lunch or dinner. It would be perfect for Christmas Eve as part of the Seven Fishes tradition.

> 7 tablespoons olive oil, divided
> 12 oz. sea scallops
> 12 oz. shrimp, shelled and deveined
> 2 teaspoons fresh lemon juice
> 1 lb. cod fillets, cut into cubes
> 1 tablespoon sugar
> l tablespoon minced dry onion
> 1 teaspoon salt
> ½ teaspoon garlic powder
> ½ teaspoon black pepper
> ½ teaspoon red pepper flakes
> 1 cup fresh basil leaves, divided
> 1 6-oz. can small pitted ripe olives, drained
> 1 5¾-oz. jar pimiento-stuffed Spanish green
>   olives, drained
> 1 4½-oz. jar artichoke hearts, drained
> 8 oz. mushroom caps, cleaned and sliced
> 12 oz. mozzarella, cut into l-inch chunks
> 4 oz. cherry tomatoes cut in half
> l cup good quality olive oil
> ⅔ cup balsamic vinegar
> crisp salad greens
> basil leaves for garnish

Heat 4 tablespoons olive oil in large non-stick skillet over high heat. Add scallops; cook and stir 2 to 4 minutes until scallops are opaque. Remove from heat. Add shrimp to the pan, and cook about 5 minutes or until the shrimp turn opaque and are firm to the touch. Combine the shrimp and scallops, and stir in the lemon juice. Set aside.

Heat remaining 3 tablespoons olive oil in another large non-stick skillet over high heat. Add cod, and cook, stirring, 1 to 2 minutes until cod is opaque. Remove from heat. Set aside.

Combine sugar, onion, salt, garlic powder, black pepper, and red pepper flakes in small bowl. Place ½ cup basil leaves in bottom of a 13x9 inch dish, sprinkle with half the sugar mixture. Add seafood, layer olives, mushrooms, artichokes, and cheese over seafood. Top with remaining sugar mixture and ½ cup basil leaves. Combine olive oil and vinegar; pour over basil and seafood mixture.

Cover and refrigerate overnight. To serve, discard top layer of basil leaves. Using slotted spoon, remove seafood mixture from pan. Discard bottom layer of basil leaves. Place seafood mixture on a platter lined with greens. Garnish if desired.

According to the "Southern Italy expert" at the Italian consulate in Philadelphia, the Seven Fishes is a tradition still kept in southern Italy. I'm told they serve thirteen dishes, seven of which should be fish. And the fish are baccala, calamari, eel, mussels, clams, sardines and octopus... but we still don't know why.

MAKES 12 SERVINGS

Roasted Olives

olive arrostite

When I was a young girl my grandmother would tell me stories about her childhood adventures in Terravecchia, a small hilltown in Calabria. She spoke to me often about climbing the olive trees on her parents' property. It was her job in the late fall to shake the branches of the trees to encourage the ripe olives to fall into the nets lying below. The olives would later be gathered and taken into town to be pressed into the oil that the family used for cooking throughout the year.

Grandma Tursi always had black olives on her table. I offer you this recipe that uses assorted olives. I hope you will always have some olives on your table, too.

> 3 cups assorted black and green olives
> zest of one orange
> ¼ teaspoon dried chili flakes
> 2 rosemary sprigs, stripped of their leaves
> ¼ -⅓ cup olive oil
> salt and pepper to taste

Preheat oven to 400°. In a bowl, combine all ingredients. Toss together to coat the olives well. Put the olives on a roasting pan and roast for 10 minutes. Serve warm or at room temperature.

Olives may be kept refrigerated for several days. Return to room temperature before serving.

MAKES 24 SERVINGS

Melon Prosciutto

prosciutto e melone

This appetizer is a classic. It is perfect before any meal, and especially nice on a warm summer evening, accompanied by a bottle of well-chilled Prosecco.

> ½ lb. prosciutto, thinly sliced
> 1 large cantaloupe or honeydew melon

Trim fat from prosciutto. Cut melon into balls. Wrap a slice of prosciutto around each melon ball. Insert a frilled toothpick to hold pieces together. Arrange on a pretty platter.

MAKES 8 SERVINGS

Artichoke Spread

> 1 14-oz. can artichoke hearts
> 1 cup mayonnaise
> 1 cup grated Parmesan cheese
> crackers or crostini

Drain artichoke hearts and pull them apart. Blend all ingredients together. Place in a greased Pyrex pie pan and bake at 350° for 20 minutes or until bubbly. Serve hot with crackers or crostini.

MAKES 8 SERVINGS

Polenta with Goat Cheese and Sun-Dried Tomatoes

polenta con formaggio di capra e pomodori

My roots go back to Calabria in Southern Italy, where pasta is served regularly with tomato sauces. My friend Lynn Matte Gibbs was raised in the traditions of Northern Italy, where polenta is a staple, and it was she who introduced me to it.

Polenta is easy to make. Just add the cornmeal slowly to the salted water while stirring. Patience is required, however, because you must continue to stir the mixture for 30 minutes while the cornmeal thickens.

When served soft, directly from the pot, polenta is an excellent accompaniment to stews such as Angello alla Cacciatora. It can also be spread out on a sheet to cool, at which time it can be cut into squares and baked or grilled.

6 oz. goat cheese with herbs, crumbled
3 to 4 tablespoons milk or half and half
12 slices firm polenta, about ¾ inch thick
1 tablespoon extra-virgin olive oil
sun dried tomatoes

Preheat oven to 350°. Combine goat cheese and milk in a bowl. Arrange polenta slices on a lightly-oiled baking sheet, and top each piece with the milk-and-cheese mixture and a strip of sun-dried tomato. Bake for ten minutes, or until polenta is heated through.

Use pre-made polenta rolls in this recipe, or make your own polenta, following package directions and adding 1 cup Parmesan cheese while cooking. You can cut different shapes from the sheet of polenta, depending on the occasion—for example, hearts for the feast of San Valentino.

MAKES 12 SERVINGS

Marinated Artichokes and Mushrooms

marinata di carciofi e funghi

Nothing could be easier to make than this dish. Add some sliced Italian meats and cheeses and you have a complete antipasto tray.

½ cup olive oil
2 tablespoons wine vinegar
½ teaspoon salt
freshly-ground pepper
1 small garlic clove, minced
1 bay leaf
1 can artichoke hearts
1 8-oz. package mushrooms, cleaned and sliced

Combine olive oil, vinegar, salt, pepper, minced garlic and bay leaf. Pour over artichokes and sliced mushrooms. Marinate for at least 6 hours in the refrigerator. Drain and pour artichokes and mushrooms into a glass bowl.

MAKES 6 SERVINGS

Soups

Soup is often served at the Italian table as the *primi* or first course of a meal. Italians love their food and, in the cool months, they especially like to start their meal with a hearty bowl of steaming soup. However, soup is enjoyed all year long, not only as a starter, but also as a satisfying lunch or dinner. With the addition of a crisp green salad, some crusty bread, a wedge of cheese, and fresh fruit, the meal is complete.

This section introduces a sampling of soups that we frequently enjoy in our family. Beginning with good rich stocks, you can make and enjoy Nonna's *Stracciatella*—a soup my grandmother made frequently. As a youngster I recall watching the chicken stock bubbling away in her well-worn soup pot. Nonna would take a few eggs with a handful of Parmesan cheese and beat them until they were light and fluffy. With her big soup spoon she would make a whirlpool in the soup and then slowly pour the egg and cheese mixture into the pot. The eggs would form small thread like strands, and after simmering for just a minute or two, Nonna would ladle our soup into bowls and sprinkle fresh parsley and more cheese over the top. This was such comforting food, especially when we were suffering from a winter cold.

The Italian Wedding Soup is an heirloom recipe so delicious it is reserved for special occasions such as holidays, birthdays, or weddings. The rich stock filled with chicken, marble sized meatballs that were laboriously rolled out by the family, spinach, and ring-shaped pasta easily made a full meal.

During a recent trip to Italy, I visited my friend Doris Fortino and her husband Doug Haynes. Arriving on a cold and cloudy January afternoon at their villa, Il Mulino, in Tofori, outside of Lucca, I was welcomed with a hearty bowl of *Tortellini in Brodo di Fagioli*. Drizzled with olive oil from their own olives, the soup is immensely satisfying.

Then there is my sons' favorite, Hamburger Vegetable Soup. When they were quite young I had a difficult time getting them to eat their vegetables, but when I served this hearty soup, the bowls were practically licked clean. In my own home, I keep a pot of *Brodo di Pomodori* on the stove or crock-pot all winter long. In the cold months it is a soothing elixir and a wonderful way to warm guests who have come in from outdoors. At Christmas it is beautiful served in white soup cups with a ring of freshly snipped parsley. Served chilled in the warm months of summer, it is a refreshing *primi*.

Soup stock

A good soup stock is the most important ingredient in many soups. Without a rich stock your soup can be flavorless. My good friend and chef Lido Martini of Fattoria Gambaro, in Petrogano, Italy, tells me that the first thing they make at a restaurant when it opens for the day is a soup stock. If your trattoria serves seafood, you would begin with a rich seafood stock. If the restaurant serves meat dishes then meat stocks are prepared. These stocks are not only used for soups, but in sauces and to deglaze pans. It may not always be possible for you to have a soup stock bubbling away, so I suggest that when you make your stock, you freeze it in small portions to have ready-at-hand when you need it.

Lido tells his class that you must begin to cook your meat parts in cold water. As the water gradually heats the meat, vegetables, and herbs, they will release their flavors into the water, giving you a rich stock. Begin with hot water and you will seal the juices of the meat, and the result is a watery stock.

Chicken Stock

brodo di pollo

¼ cup cooking oil
3-4 lb. chicken, cut up
4 cups yellow onions, chopped
2 cups carrots, chopped
2 cups celery, chopped
handful fresh parsley
3 quarts cold water, adding more as needed
1 tablespoon dried thyme
4 bay leaves
3 tablespoons chicken stock base

Pour the oil into a large heavy stock pot and heat. Pat the chicken parts dry with a paper towel and drop them into the hot oil. Toss and turn them until they are well-browned—about 15 minutes. Add onions, carrot, celery, and continue to cook, stirring frequently, until vegetables begin to brown and lose their crunch. Add remaining ingredients, using enough water to cover solids by at least 2 inches, and bring stock to a boil.

Boil vigorously for 15 minutes, skimming off all scum. Reduce heat, cover, and simmer briskly for 2 hours, skimming scum from time to time as necessary.

Cool the stock; then pour through a strainer set over a bowl, pressing hard on the vegetable and chicken parts with the back of a spoon to extract as much flavor as possible. Cover and refrigerate overnight.

Skim any congealed fat from the stock before using. Transfer defatted stock to storage containers, label, and freeze for later use.

MAKES ABOUT 3 QUARTS

Beef Stock

brodo di manzo

4 to 5 lb. beef chuck or shoulder,
   cut into pieces
7 quarts cold water
1½ tablespoons salt
10 black peppercorns
1 bay leaf
8 whole cloves
2 large onions, chopped into large pieces
2 carrots, chopped into large pieces
3 ribs celery, chopped into large pieces
3 tablespoons beef stock base

Place the beef, water, salt, pepper, bay leaves, cloves, vegetables, and beef stock base into a large stockpot and heat to boiling. Skim off the scum that comes to the top.

Continue to simmer for 3-4 hours uncovered, skimming the top frequently. If necessary, add a bit more water. Cool the stock and strain. Store in the refrigerator for 1 week or in the freezer for up to 2 months.

MAKES ABOUT 7 QUARTS

Nonna's Stracciatella

stracciattella della nonna

Nonna would make this soup frequently. I loved to eat it, but I also loved to watch her pour the egg mixture into the bubbling soup. When I make this soup now I think fond thoughts of my special Nonna.

1 quart chicken broth
2 eggs
2 tablespoons freshly grated Parmesan
 cheese
2 teaspoons finely chopped fresh parsley
zest of a lemon
salt (if necessary)
olive oil (optional)

In a small bowl, beat the eggs until they are blended, then mix in the cheese, parsley, and lemon zest. Bring the chicken stock to a vigorous boil in a heavy pot. Pour in the egg mixture, stirring gently with a wire whisk. Simmer, still stirring, for 2 minutes; the egg will form small flakes. Pour into a heated tureen and serve in a bowl, topped with more parsley and cheese, and a drizzle of olive oil.

To fortify the soup, add 2 tablespoons of breadcrumbs and 1 tablespoon of flour to to the egg mixture, and mix well. Then follow the recipe above.

MAKES 4 SERVINGS

Italian Sausage Soup

zuppa di salsiccia

My aunt Darlene Torri Tursi is an excellent cook, and you would have to be to fill up the likes of my uncle Paul and their five children. It is important to use a rich beef stock for this recipe. Aunt Dar uses bowtie pasta, or *farfalle* (butterflies), as the Italians call it, but other pasta could also be used. I recommend a mild or medium sausage for this recipe.

1 lb. Italian sausage
2 cloves garlic, chopped
1 large onion, chopped
1 28-oz. can Italian plum tomatoes,
 chopped
2½ quarts beef stock
¾ cup dry red wine
1½ tablespoons minced parsley
1 teaspoon dried basil
½ green pepper, chopped
2 cups bowtie pasta, cooked
Parmesan cheese

Break up sausage as you brown it along with the garlic and onion. When meat is browned, drain off excess fat. Add tomatoes, beef stock, wine, parsley, and basil. Simmer for 30 minutes, stirring occassionally. Add green pepper and cook 15 minutes more. Add cooked pasta to the hot soup. Top with the grated Parmesan cheese.

MAKES 8 SERVINGS

Italian Wedding Soup

minestra maritata

Italian wedding soup is usually served as a *primi* course for special occasions. I find that it is a great soup to make as a family activity. Don't let the many steps of this soup deter you from making it; instead, assign tasks to groups. Let one group make and roll out the marble-sized meatballs while another group chops the vegetables. Then assemble the soup and enjoy it together.

I especially like to use fresh spinach in this soup; with the chopped tomatoes, it is very colorful and appealing.

1 whole chicken, about 4 lb; rinsed and dried
1 large onion, chopped
5 stalks celery, chopped
handful of parsley, chopped
⅓ lb. each of ground veal, pork, and beef
2 tablespoons of grated Romano cheese
    plus extra
2 slices day old bread
½ cup milk
1 egg beaten
salt and freshly ground pepper
4 cups chicken broth
5 carrots, peeled and chopped
1 28-oz. can chopped tomatoes
1 10-oz. package frozen
chopped spinach or 1 lb. fresh,
    washed and chopped
1 cup cooked ring-shaped pasta

Place the chicken, celery, and onion in a large pot. Fill the pot with cold water and bring it to a simmer. Cover the pot and cook for 1½ hours, skimming any foam off the top.

To prepare the meatballs, combine the ground meat, beaten egg, handful of chopped parsley, cheese, and salt and pepper to taste. Squeeze out the breadcrumbs, and add to the meat mixture. Mix until well combined. Oil the palms of your hands and roll out meatballs into the size of marbles and place on a well-greased cookie sheet. Bake meatballs 10 to 15 minutes in a 350° oven. Drain meatballs and set them aside until ready to assemble soup.

Remove the chicken from the pot and strain the liquid. Discard the onion and the celery. Pour this stock back into the pot and add the canned chicken broth and tomatoes with their juices. (Adding the canned broth to the homemade stock fortifies the soup.) Bring the soup to a boil.

Remove the meat from the chicken when cool enough to handle. Chop the meat from the cooked chicken and add it to the pot along with the carrots and meatballs. Season with salt and pepper to taste, and simmer for another 10 minutes.

Meanwhile, cook pasta in a separate pot. Add the cooked pasta and the spinach to the soup and simmer for a few more minutes. Serve with grated Pecorino cheese.

MAKES 12 SERVINGS

Il Mulino, Tofori, Italy

Tortellini in Bean Soup

tortellini in brodo di fagioli

Tortellini in Brodo di Fagioli is actually two soups, a tortellini soup and a bean soup. Served separately each is very good, but together they are spectacular. My friend Doris Fortino first served this soup to us when we arrived at her Tuscan villa, Il Mulino, one cold, rainy, January day. The fire was roaring in the huge fireplace, but it was this hearty soup that warmed us. Served with a salad, crusty Italian bread, and a glass of good wine, you have a complete meal.

For the bean soup:

   ¾ lb. cannellini beans
   1 clove garlic
   salt, pepper
   4-5 sage leaves
   1 shallot
   1 carrot
   1 stalk celery
   3 peeled tomatoes
   olive oil

For the meat stock:

   1 lb. beef shoulder
   ½ stewing chicken
   1 red onion
   1 carrot
   5 peeled tomatoes
   1 stalk celery
   small bunch fresh basil
   salt, pepper
   olive oil

For the bean soup: soak the beans in 3 quarts of water overnight. Drain and cook the beans with garlic, salt, pepper, and a few sage leaves, on a stem for easy removal later. Cook for about an hour, until the beans are soft but not mushy.

While beans are cooking, mince the shallot, carrots, celery, and tomatoes finely, and then sauté them in a little oil for 5 minutes. Add cooked beans to the mixture and purée. Simmer slowly for another 30 minutes.

For the meat stock: place meat, vegetables, and salt in cold water to cover, at least 2 quarts.

Boil for about 2 hours. Strain stock, remove meat and vegetables, and bring the stock back to a boil.

For the tortellini:

   1 lb. fresh pasta in sheets

For the filling:

   ¼ lb. ground pork
   ¼ lb. ground veal
   ¼ lb. mortadella
   2 oz. minced prosciutto
   1 link Italian sausage, cooked
   1 egg
   4 oz. Parmesan cheese
   1 pat butter

In a frying pan, sauté the pork, veal, and sausage in butter until browned. Finely chop the mortadella, sausage, and prosciutto. Mix together and allow meat mixture to cool. Then add the egg, nutmeg, and Parmesan, adjust salt and mix well to a fine moist mixture.

Cut two-inch squares of pasta. Place a small quantity of filling in the center. Fold into triangle shape and fold outer points together and squeeze to from tortellini shape.

Bring meat stock to a boil. Add tortellini and cook until it floats to the top—about 3 or 4 minutes. In a bowl, ladle in bean soup at a porportion of 1 ladle of bean soup to two ladels of stock with tortellini. Serve hot.

MAKES 8 SERVINGS

Grandma Torri's Tortellini Soup

zuppa di tortellini di nonna torri

I can remember as a very young girl, watching my grandmother, mother, and aunts working in my grandmother's "basement kitchen." In those days all of the Italian families had two kitchens. One kitchen was used for eating and making the final preparations of a meal. The real work was done in the "basement kitchen," where there was room for many people to work. The lamb was slaughtered for Easter dinner there, the bread for the week was baked, the pasta was rolled and cut, and the tortellini were stuffed with the meat mixture.

Near the holidays you would find the women of my family making my Aunt Darlene's recipe for tortellini. Her Nonna Torri, from the northern part of Italy, had given her the recipe, and it is this recipe that my family still uses today. I hope you will enjoy it for your next holiday.

For the Tortellini:

2 chicken breasts (boil and grind meat)
2 slices lean pork, about 8 oz. (grind raw)
small onion, chopped
1 clove garlic, minced
2 eggs
¾ cup bread crumbs
2 tablespoons grated Parmesan cheese
pinch nutmeg
pinch allspice
salt and pepper

For the chicken broth, boil:

a whole chicken or 2 large breasts and a soup bone
1 cup chopped celery
1 cup chopped onion
salt, pepper
1 tablespoon tomato paste

Let simmer 2 hours. When done simmering, strain. Return broth to the pot.

Boil the chicken and grind the meat. Grind the pork raw, then brown it with a small chopped onion and a clove of garlic that has been minced. Mix the meat with eggs, bread crumbs, cheese, and spices. You may chill the mixture at this point.

Make your favorite pasta dough and roll out very thin, using a pasta machine. Cut the dough into 2-inch squares. Fill the squares with meat and fold over to make a triangle, pinch ends using a fork to seal. Let these dry out and then freeze if you are making ahead.

For the soup:

Let chicken broth come to a boil and add tortellini. Cook tortellini in the broth until they float to the top. Ladle out into warm bowls and add freshly-ground cheese and a sprinkle of fresh parsley.

This soup is a holiday tradition. The tortellini can be made several days ahead and frozen.

MAKES 8 SERVINGS

Turkey Spinach Soup

zuppa di spinaci e tacchino

Turkey spinach soup was one of the favorite items on our menu at Occasions Catering. My partner Marla came up with the recipe one year and we have been enjoying it ever since. This soup is a great way to use up Thanksgiving leftovers.

¼ cup butter
2 medium onions, chopped
2 tablespoons flour
1 teaspooon curry powder
3 cups chicken broth
1 cup diced potatoes
½ cup thin-sliced carrots
½ cup sliced celery
2 tablespoons chopped fresh parsley
½ teaspoon dried sage
2 cups cooked turkey
1½ cups half and half
1 10-oz. package frozen spinach (or 1 lb. fresh)
salt and pepper

Melt butter in a soup pot over medium heat. Add onions and sauté for about 10 minutes. Stir in flour and curry powder and cook 2 to 3 minutes. Add broth, potatoes, carrots, celery, parsley, and sage, and bring to a boil.

Reduce heat to low, cover, and simmer for 10 minutes. Add turkey, half and half, and spinach. Cover and simmer until heated through. Add salt and pepper.

MAKES 8 SERVINGS

Lentil or Split Pea Soup

zuppa di lenticchie

If it was Friday and Lent you can be sure that we would be having lentil soup for supper. This is my mother Sarah Fazio Tursi's recipe for *Zuppa di Lenticchie*. Mom drizzles a bit of olive oil over each bowl just before serving.

I like to purée the soup. For a more festive *primi* course, pour a tablespoon of dry sherry on the top instead of the olive oil.

1 lb. dried lentils or split peas
½ cup diced onions
½ cup diced carrots
½ cup diced celery
1 garlic clove, chopped
salt and pepper to taste

Rinse and sort through the peas. In a large pot, add peas to 6-8 cups of water. Bring to a rapid boil and boil for about 2 minutes. Skim off the scum that forms on the top and discard. Add onions, celery, carrots, and garlic to the pot and simmer for about 1½ hours. You will need to add more water as it cooks.

When ready to serve, pour into a heated soup bowl and drizzle with olive oil.

One can of chopped tomatoes and some small cooked pasta can also be added.

MAKES 8 SERVINGS

Fish Stew

zuppa di pesce

If you can't visit the Amalfi or Ligurian coast of Italy to enjoy the seafood of the area, then make your own *Zuppa di Pesce*, or fish stew. Just make sure you are using the freshest ingredients you can find.

½ cup onion, chopped
½ cup green pepper, chopped
2 garlic cloves, minced
1 tablespoon olive oil
1 teaspoon salt
½ teaspoon freshly ground pepper
1 lb. fresh shrimp, shells removed
    and deveined
1 quart diced tomatoes, plus juice
2 8-oz. bottles clam juice
1 cup dry white wine
1 6½-oz. can minced clams
1½ teaspoons grated lemon rind
¼ cup freshly chopped parsley

Sauté onion, peppers, and garlic in oil in a large pot until soft. Add salt and pepper.

Stir in tomatoes, clam juice, and wine. Bring to a boil, lower heat, and simmer for five minutes. Add shrimp and clams, and simmer until shrimp are tender, about five minutes. Stir in lemon rind and parsley and serve hot. (Do not boil.)

MAKES 8 SERVINGS

Hamburger Vegetable Soup

zuppa di verdure e manzo

An all-time family favorite, this soup was the only way I could get my boys, Brian, Patrick, and Teddy, to eat their vegetables. They are adults now, but they still request it time and again. I will make a batch of this easy soup and freeze it in serving-sized containers for them to enjoy at home. They may live far away, but when they dip into this soup they think they're still in my warm cucina.

1 lb. best quality ground beef
1 cup chopped onions
¼ teaspoon salt
1½ cups chopped celery
1 cup thinly sliced carrots
2 cups potatoes, peeled and diced
4 beef bouillon cubes
1 14-oz. can diced tomatoes
1 10-oz. package frozen mixed vegetables
1 bay leaf
¼ teaspoon pepper
4 cups hot water

In a large kettle, brown the ground beef, sprinkling with salt while browning. Stir in the remaining ingredients. Bring to a boil. Simmer, covered, until vegetables are tender-crisp, about 30 minutes.

MAKES 8 SERVINGS

Tomato Soup

brodo di pomodori

This light soup makes a very nice *primi* course, especially at Christmas. It can also be made in a crockpot and kept warm for several hours. In the winter it's a wonderful way to warm up when you have been out in the cold.

3 cups vegetable tomato juice
2 cups chicken stock
2 tablespoons light brown sugar
2 tablespoons butter
parsley, finely chopped

Combine the vegetable tomato juice, chicken stock, brown sugar, and butter. Let simmer for about 10 minutes. Serve in cups or soup bowls.

MAKES 8 SERVINGS

bread and
pizza

My son Brian provided these reminiscences of my grandmother, which I now share with you.

My great grandmother, Anna Fazio, was one of the most loving and faithful Italian women ever. She was never without a rosary in her hand, always at the front row of the church, and as quick to give her great grandchildren a dollar or candy as a hug upon seeing them. One of the greatest gifts grandma ever gave us, however, was her bread recipe and ritual.

Despite being a widow living on her own, grandma's house never felt empty. She surrounded herself with statues and icons of the saints, Jesus, Mary and Joseph and photos of her large family. The whole scene was frequently permeated with the scent of freshly baked or baking bread.

One day in my youth my parents thought it would be in my interest—and provide them with a day of sanity—if I learned the family bread recipe with Nana. They dropped me off the night before our baking day, as the ritual began early in the morning. I spent some time talking with Nana and watching a television variety show before being tucked into bed under the watchful eye of her saint statues—some of which glowed eerily in the dark.

I awoke before dawn to the pitter patter of Nana's feet setting the kitchen for work. I rubbed my eyes and sauntered out to her pantry to find breakfast. We sat down together before a steaming pot of coffee and bowls of cereal. After a quick blessing, I was stunned to watch Nana pour her coffee over her Raisin Bran and begin to eat. Not fully understanding what Nana was up to, and not wanting to be rude, I ate my cereal dry. Then it was right to work. I saw flour, yeast, and other ingredients displayed around a large mixing bowl, but I was at a loss about how we were going to measure out these ingredients. But for Nana, to whom the ritual was second nature, measuring devices would only crowd the work space. Amazingly, she measured out the ingredients using pinches, palms and handfuls of ingredients, cooking from instinct. It wasn't until years later that the actual recipe was written down when my father insisted that Nana throw her dashes, pinches, and handfuls of ingredients into measuring cups and spoons.

Our dough complete, the muscle work began. Despite being a petite woman, Nana would give the dough a thrashing that wowed me. Strength can be found in the places we least

My grandparents, Anna and Joe Fazio

place. She seemed contented in these moments and the rare times she was unhappy or perturbed by something, she would dismiss with a disgruntled wave of her hand—extending from under her chin and outward—and a little grunt.

Then, when the time had passed, it was back to work, molding the dough into baking form. In accordance with an Italian legend Nana would split the top of each loaf to let the "bad spirits" (yeast perhaps?) out of each loaf, protecting those who would later eat with her. In addition to bread, she formed pizza crusts and rolls, and then baked them up into something delicious.

Few of her grandchildren participated in this ritual with her, but they always had an uncanny ability to show up as a hot loaf or loaded pizza was pulled from the oven. It struck me as if this—a visit from those she loved—was the answer to Nana's silent prayers during the time of preparation and waiting, serving as the reward for her work and patience.

Please enjoy preparing the following recipes with and for those who are special in your life. — *Brian Hobbins*

expect it; there was amazing power in Nana's kneading. The dough properly worked over, she then quietly placed the heap in a plastic bowl and covered it with a towel and sat on her couch to wait for the next step. In addition to her strength, Nana was amazingly patient and would wait for hours for the dough to rise to double its size before beating it back down and letting it rise again. In that time, she would quietly visit, say a decade of the rosary, or even just stare off as if in a memory or another

Italian Bread

il pane

I share with you my maternal grandmother Anna Fazio's bread recipe. From this recipe came the loaves of bread that we slathered with butter; the pitas that we dipped in sugar; and the loaded pizzas we all enjoyed. On the feast of St. Joseph, grandma would make small rolls from the dough to celebrate the feast of San Giuseppe.

    4 packages dry yeast
    5-6 cups warm water
    5 teaspoons salt
    2 tablespoons sugar
    5 lb. of flour
    ½ cup shortening

Dissolve yeast in water; add shortening, salt, and sugar. Make a well in the center of the flour in a large pan. Add all the other ingredients. Knead dough until smooth and elastic (10-15 minutes). Add more water if needed. Let rise until double in size, at least 2 hours. Punch dough down, then form into 5 balls. Let the balls rise for an hour. Form each ball into a loaf and slash the tops, making slashes every 3 inches.

Preheat oven to 400°. Place the loaves on cookie sheets and bake 15 minutes. Turn sheets and continue baking for another 45 minutes or so. When bread is golden brown, remove from oven and cool on rack.

MAKES 5 LOAVES

Fried Bread

pita fritta

One of my fondest childhood memories is of sitting at the table at my Grandma Tursi's basement kitchen. She would have been baking bread all morning. Grandma would call my brother Frank and me in, and she would fry us *pita frittas* with the dough she had reserved. As they came out of the hot oil, Frank and I would let them cool off just for a moment, so we could handle them. Then we would each break off a piece and dip it into the sugar bowl. Today, it makes me hungry just to think about it.

    1 loaf of Grandma's bread dough
    oil for frying
    sugar

Break off some of the dough—the amount you would use if you were making buns. Stretch it out into a 5-6 inch circle. Put a hole in the middle of it.

Heat a small amount of oil in a frying pan. When it's hot, drop in the dough. Fry on both sides until golden brown. Drain on paper towels. While still hot, dip into the sugar. Best if eaten warm.

MAKES 12 SERVINGS

Easter Bread

pane di pasqualino

It was always a sure sign of spring when my mother's beautiful *Pane de Pasqualina* appeared. The colored eggs intertwined in the braids are a symbol of the renewal that we experience at this time of the year.

5 lb. flour plus 1 cup
3 teaspoons anise seed (optional)
6 eggs, beaten
2 cups milk
2 cups water
½ stick butter, softened
½ cup oil
4 packages dry yeast
5 teaspoons salt
5 teaspoons sugar
3-5 eggs

In a large bowl, mix flour and anise seed together. Scald milk and water, let cool, and then add yeast. Add eggs to flour, then add the butter and oil, and finally, add the liquid with yeast. Add sugar and salt. Knead the bread mixture until elastic—it may need a little more water. Cover the bowl, and put in a warm place.

Let the dough rest for about an hour. Knead again for about 10 minutes, and let rest again for about an hour. Divide dough into 15 balls and roll each ball into a rope about 25 inches long. Take three ropes and braid them together.

On a greased cookie sheet, form the braid into a ring. Cover and let rise until double in size, about an hour. Brush with melted butter and bake at 375° for about 40 minutes.

Colored eggs may be inserted between the braids. As the bread bakes, the eggs will also bake in their shells. Using an odd number of eggs will give a more pleasing look.

MAKES 5 LOAVES

Patrick Hobbins making taralli with
grandparents Joe and Sarah Tursi

Pretzels with Anise Seeds

taralli

Grandma Tursi made these frequently. I would
watch her first plunge them into boiling water,
and then bake them until they were golden brown.
I would wait until they were cool enough to handle
but still warm, and then slather them with butter
and eat. But taralli are good to eat anytime and
with just about anything!

3 cups warm tap water
1½ packages dry yeast
½ stick butter, plus 2 tablespoons
3½ teaspoons salt
3 teaspoons sugar
2 eggs, beaten
3 lb. flour
2 teaspoons or more of anise seeds

Mix first 6 ingredients together. Then add flour
and work until smooth. (Add a little more water if
necessary.) Let rest 15 minutes. Form into a ball,
and knead for at least 10 minutes. Then cut the
dough into smaller balls and let rest in plastic bags
for 15 minutes. (Refrigerate dough if weather is
very warm.)

Cut pieces the size of a large tablespoon off of
a ball of dough, and roll into a 6-inch rope. Form
into a circle and pinch ends together. Plunge into
boiling water. When taralli surface to the top,
remove from the pot. Place on ungreased cookie
sheets and bake at 375° for about 20 minutes.

*To keep crisp, put in a cookie jar. Storing them in plastic
will make them soft.*

MAKES ABOUT 12 DOZEN

Panini

Panini are the sandwiches of Italy. They can be served cold or toasted for a hot sandwich. If you do not own a panini maker, this might be a good time to purchase one. It will make even the most ordinary sandwiches delicious.

Italian Artichoke and Cheese Sandwich

panini con carciofi e formaggio

1 cup quartered marinated artichoke hearts, drained
6 thin slices part-skim mozzarella cheese
1 loaf Italian bread, cut length-wise and scooped out
salt and pepper
1 red or green pepper, sliced
2 tablespoons fresh parsley
1 tablespoon lemon juice
2 tablespoons olive oil
salad greens

Layer artichokes and cheese on bottom of loaf. Sprinkle with salt and pepper. Top with peppers, parsley, and lemon juice. Sprinkle with olive oil. Top with salad greens.

Replace top half of bread. Wrap in plastic. Let stand 30 minutes, then slice.

MAKES 6–8 SERVINGS

Italian Panini Sandwich

Panini all'Itaniana

I suggest you use the best imported meats and cheeses from an Italian deli when making this classic panini.

  1 round loaf focaccia
  ½ cup Italian salad dressing (below)
  Italian meats such as proscuitto,
      salami, or mortadella
  Provolone cheese, sliced thin
  ½ cup sliced roasted peppers, drained
  ½ red onion, thinly sliced
  4 sliced roma tomatoes
  salt and pepper
  2 cups chopped romaine lettuce

Italian salad dressing
  ¾ cup olive oil
  ¼ cup balsamic vinegar
  salt and pepper to taste

Split focaccia in half. Sprinkle each half with salad dressing. Layer meats and cheese. Top with peppers, onion, tomatoes, and lettuce. Drizzle with any remaining dressing. Replace top half of loaf. Wrap tightly in plastic wrap and let stand for 30 minutes. Slice into wedges.

You can substitute your favorite Italian salad dressing for this panini.

MAKES 8 SERVINGS

Portobello Mushroom Sandwiches

panini con funghi portobello

I love portobello mushrooms. This recipe, in which the mushrooms are topped with herbed goat cheese, a perfectly ripe tomato, and basil leaves, is divine. Use small focaccia if available when making this panini.

  2 tablespoons balsamic vinegar
  1 tablespoon extra-virgin olive oil
  4 portobello mushroom caps
  basil leaves
  3 oz. herbed goat cheese
  4 large rolls such as focaccia
  4 slices ripe tomato
  lettuce leaves

Mix balsamic vinegar and olive oil; then brush on the mushrooms. Heat grill or grill pan to medium. Grill mushrooms for 3 minutes, turn, brush with mixture again. Then grill another 2 minutes.

Slice goat cheese into rounds. With the bottoms of the mushrooms up, place a slice on each mushroom cap. Toast rolls for 3 minutes while continuing to grill mushrooms. Remove rolls and mushrooms from grill.

Place a mushroom on bottom of a roll, top with basil leaf, tomato slice, and lettuce. Use any desired condiments. Top with other half of roll.

MAKES 4 SERVINGS

Easy Focaccia

focaccia con erbe aromatiche

Focaccias are found all over Italy, and they are a favorite food of the Italians. The choice of toppings is a matter for the cook to decide. A few simple options are described at right.

1 loaf frozen bread dough
dried Italian herbs
1 clove garlic, minced
red pepper flakes
¼ cup freshly grated Parmesan cheese
olive oil

Thaw dough according to package directions. Oil a 9 x 13 glass baking dish well. Put olive oil on your hands and drizzle some on the bread. Stretch the dough to fit the pan. Sprinkle with minced garlic, dried Italian herbs, red pepper flakes, and Parmesan cheese. Bake in a hot 350° oven for about 30 minutes. Let cool slightly. Cut into strips with a pizza cutter.

MAKES 12 SERVINGS

1) Tomato Topping

1 cup drained sun-dried tomatoes, or peeled
**   fresh tomatoes**
1 teaspoon dried Italian herbs
¼ cup grated Parmesan cheese

Mix ingredients, sprinkle over focaccia, and bake.

2) Onion Topping

2 lb. sweet onions, sliced thin
3 tablespoons olive oil

Cook onions for 30 minutes in oil. Cool. Top focaccia with onions, and bake. (For an unusual taste, add ½ cup of chopped sun-dried tomatoes to the onions before serving.)

3) Roasted Red Pepper and Goat Cheese

1½ cups roasted red peppers,
**   cut into ¼ inch strips**
olive oil
salt
¾ cup goat cheese

Top focaccia with red pepper strips, drizzle with olive oil and sprinkle with salt. Bake for 15 minutes in a moderate oven. Remove from oven, sprinkle with the goat cheese, and return to oven until cheese melts.

Pesto Focaccia

focaccia al pesto

Boboli pizza crust
Di Giorno pesto or your own homemade pesto
4 oz. package feta cheese crumbles
3 diced tomatoes, seeds removed

Spread pesto on the pizza crust. Sprinkle with feta cheese and diced tomatoes. Bake at 400° for about 20 minutes.

If there is extra olive oil on top of the focaccia after it is baked, soak up the excess with a paper towel before serving.

MAKES 8 SERVINGS

Grilled Vegetable Focaccia

focaccia con verdure grigliatte

2 large yellow or red bell peppers,
    seeded and quartered
1 medium eggplant, thinly sliced
1 large onion, sliced
8 oz. sliced mushrooms
4 tablespoons olive oil
1½ tablespoons balsamic vinegar
1 10-12 inch focaccia
2 tablespoons Italian salad dressing
½ cup grated Parmesan cheese
½ cup shredded Romaine lettuce
½ cup chopped Roma tomatoes

Combine vegetables with oil and vinegar in a large self-sealing bag, and shake well to coat. Grill vegetables on a pre-heated grill and baste with marinade from bag for 15 minutes.

Split focaccia and spread grilled vegetables onto bottom side. Drizzle Italian dressing over all and sprinkle with cheese. Place lettuce and tomatoes on top. Replace top half of focaccia, and cut into four pieces.

Ciabatta bread also works well with this topping.

MAKES 4 SERVINGS

Pizza Dough

pasta per pizza

My Italian tutor and friend Daniela Ruggerio shared this pizza dough recipe with me. Daniela is orginially from Naples where pizza was created. Through her business, Via Scarlotti, named after a famous Neapolitan street, Daniela works to promote the language and cuisine of Italy.

2 ⅔ cups flour
1 tablespoon olive oil
pinch of salt
1 package dry yeast
1 cup very warm milk or water

Put the flour in a deep bowl, then add the oil and salt. Mix the yeast with the almost-boiling milk or water. Pour this mixture into the bowl with the other ingredients.

Work the dough by hand until it becomes smooth. Then form it into a ball and leave it to rest for at least an hour in a warm place, such as a lightly-heated oven.

When the ball has doubled in size, spread it to the desired shape and thickness.

This is a very traditional pizza dough recipe, and as tradition demands, Daniela suggests a drizzle of olive oil over the top of the finished pizza, as is the Neapolitan custom.

MAKES 1 CRUST

Mushroom and Thyme Pizza

Pizza con Funghi e Timo

1 pizza dough (previous recipe)
    or premade crust
¼ cup chopped parsley
2 teaspoons fresh thyme, chopped
2 garlic cloves, minced
2 teaspoons olive oil
8 oz. sliced mushrooms
½ teaspoon salt
¼ teaspoon black pepper
Parmesan cheese

Combine parsley, thyme, and garlic in a bowl. Heat oil in a large pan over high heat. Add mushrooms and sauté for 5 minutes; then add parsley, thyme, and garlic mixture.

Roll out dough on a greased 12-inch pan. Top with mushroom mixture. Bake for 12-15 minutes or until pizza is nice and crispy. Remove from oven and sprinkle with 2 tablespoons parsley and Parmesan cheese.

MAKES 4 SERVINGS

Fresh Mozzarella and Herb Pizza

pizza con mozzarella e erbe aromatiche

1 cup tomato sauce
pizza dough (see previous recipe)
    or premade crust
1½ tablespoons chopped fresh oregano
    leaves
1 teaspoon chopped fresh thyme
1 teaspoon chopped fresh rosemary
1 teaspoon chopped fresh basil, with
    additional leaves for garnish
1 lb. fresh buffalo mozzarella, cut into ¼ inch
    slices

Spread sauce over pizza dough. Sprinkle with the fresh herbs. Arrange mozzarella slices over pizza.

Bake for 12-15 minutes in a hot 450° oven. When pizza dough is browned and crisp and cheese is golden and bubbly, remove from oven.

Cool slightly and cut into wedges.

MAKES 4 SERVINGS

57

Pizza Alfredo with Asparagus Tips

pizza con punte di asparagi e creme

pizza dough (see recipe on page 56)
        or premade crust
1½ cup whipping cream
5 oz. Romano cheese, grated
4 oz. Parmesan cheese, grated
2 dozen asparagus spears, trimmed to 4 inches
fresh ground pepper

In a heavy saucepan, bring cream to a boil over high heat. Reduce heat to low and slowly stir in the cheeses. Continue to simmer, stirring frequently, until sauce is very thick, about 10 minutes. Remove from heat.

Bring large pan of lightly salted water to a boil. Add asparagus and boil for 30 seconds. Immediately drain and rinse asparagus under cold running water until cool. Drain and pat asparagus dry.

Divide cheese sauce evenly over pizza dough. Season generously with black pepper. Arrange asparagus spears in spoke fashion over pizza with tips slightly overlapping the rim. Spoon remaining sauce over asparagus, leaving tips uncovered. Bake 8-10 minutes, or until pizza crust is brown and crisp and cheese is golden and bubbly.

MAKES 4 SERVINGS

Breakfast Pizza

pizza del mattino

This breakfast pizza is a great way to begin a weekend morning. It is nice enough to serve to guests, but your family will appreciate waking up to such a delicious meal as well.

1 loaf frozen bread dough, thawed
6 eggs, scrambled and cooled
1½ cups sliced mushrooms
½ cup chopped bell pepper
2 tablespoons chopped onion
1 cup ham, bacon, or sausage
1¼ cup shredded cheddar cheese
½ cup mozzarella cheese

Roll out dough to fit a large, greased pizza pan. Spread all ingredients over the dough in the order given. Bake at 450° for 6 to 8 minutes, or until the crust is done and cheese is melted.

For more flavor, add Italian seasonings to eggs before scrambling. Pizza can be assembled and refrigerated until you are ready to bake it.

MAKES 4 SERVINGS

Tomato, Caper, Basil, and Garlic Pizza

pizza con pomodori, capperi, basilico e aglio

pizza dough (see recipe on page 56)
    or premade crust
½ cup shredded mozzarella
4 tomatos, sliced
2 tablespoons capers
¼ cup fresh basil, chopped
½ teaspoon black pepper
¼ teaspoon salt
2 cloves garlic, minced
1 teaspoon olive oil

Stretch dough to fit a greased 12-inch pan. Sprinkle cheese on crust. Arrange tomato slices over cheese, sprinkle with capers. Bake for 15 minutes at 450°. Remove from oven. Sprinkle with basil, salt, and pepper, and drizzle with olive oil. Cut into wedges.

MAKES 4 SERVINGS

Carmelized Onion, Goat Cheese, and Arugula Pizza

*pizza con cipolle, arugula e
formaggio di capra*

pizza dough (see recipe on page 56)
    or premade crust
2 teaspoons olive oil
3 lb. thinly-sliced onions
2 teaspoons fresh rosemary, chopped
½ teaspoon salt
¼ teaspoon black pepper
3 oz. herbed goat cheese
1 cup arugula leaves

Heat oil in a large pan. Add onions and sauté for five minutes, stirring often. Add 1 teaspoon rosemary, salt, and pepper. Continue cooking 15-20 minutes, until onions are golden brown. Stir often.

Pre-heat oven to 450°. Form pizza dough, stretching it out to fill a 12-inch pan. Spread onions on top and bake 10 minutes. Add cheese and bake 5 minutes more. Remove from oven, and top with remaining rosemary and arugula. Cool slightly and cut into 4 wedges.

MAKES 4 SERVINGS

Primi Piatti

Pasta Dough

pasta fresca di Zia Elisa

My great aunt, Zia Elisa Tursi, brought this recipe with her from Italy. She used no measuring spoons or cups, so for years it was difficult for us to replicate this pasta dough. One day my cousin, Loretta Tursi Sieman, decided to get more exact measurements. Zia Elisa would pinch the salt and Loretta would pour it into measuring spoons. Zia Elisa would drop flour onto a marble table top, and then Loretta would scoop it into measuring cups. Finally, with great patience, Loretta extracted this heirloom recipe from her grandmother.

> 2½ **cups all-purpose flour**
> ⅓ **cup water**
> 2 **eggs**
> 1 **egg yolk**
> 1 **tablespoon olive oil**
> 1 **teaspoon salt**

In a large bowl, combine 1 cup flour and remaining ingredients. Mix by hand or in a mixer. Add additional flour to make a soft dough. Turn dough on a lightly-floured surface, and knead until smooth and not sticky, adding flour if necessary.

Cover dough with a towel and let rest 30 minutes. Roll out and cut dough using a pasta machine.

MAKES 1 POUND PASTA

Anna Maria Vellutini making pasta with Jan Bordonaro

61

Pasta with Herbs

pasta alla erbe

I first made this pasta sauce when going to cooking school in the Chianti region of Italy. You can use any combination of Italian herbs. Gathering the herbs in the garden of La Quercia at sunset was a beautiful experience.

> **1 cup finely chopped herbs, such as parsley, rosemany, thyme, basil, and sage**
> **3 to 4 garlic cloves, chopped**
> **¼ cup olive oil**
> **3 tablespoons tomato paste**
> **¾ to 1 cup half and half**
> **1 lb. pasta shells or campanelle pasta**
> **salt**
> **pepper**
> **1 cup Parmesan cheese**

Chop the herbs the garlic together.

Coat the bottom of a saucepan with ¼ cup olive oil. Add the herbs and garlic, and cook slowly for about 5 minutes. Slowly add the tomato paste and cook 5 minutes more. Add the half and half and whisk until blended. If the sauce seems too thick, add more half and half. Season with salt and pepper, and simmer for 5 minutes.

Meanwhile, prepare the pasta, removing from water when slightly *al dente*. Reserve 1 cup of the pasta water in case the sauce is too thick. Pour pasta into a large bowl and top with sauce, combining gently. Add reserved pasta water if necessary to loosen mixture. Toss in the cheese and continue to blend the pasta, sauce and cheese. Serve immediately and pass more cheese.

MAKES 8 SERVINGS

Pasta with Butter and Sage

pasta a burro e salvia

Use fresh sage and freshly grated cheese for this easy dish. It goes especially well with chicken or pork.

> 1 lb. farfalle (bowtie pasta)
> ½ cup unsalted butter
> 20 or more sage leaves
> ¾ cup freshly grated Parmesan cheese
> salt and pepper to taste

In a large pot bring 5 quarts of water to a boil. Add salt. Add pasta and cook according to package directions. Drain the pasta and arrange on a warm platter.

Meanwhile, melt the butter in a pan, add the sage leaves, and cook, pressing down on the leaves to release the flavor. When the butter starts to turn golden brown and the sage darkens (about 5 minutes), remove pan from heat, and pour the butter-sage sauce over the pasta. Toss well, and sprinkle with cheese. Grind some pepper over the top and serve with more cheese.

Try using other herbs, such as rosemary, basil, thyme, or a combination of the three.

MAKES 8 SERVINGS

Linguine with Pesto

linguine al pesto

I love going to the farmer's market in the summertime, when the fruits and vegetables are at their peak. This is also the time when I buy basil in great quantities, to make and freeze the pesto we'll enjoy all year long.

> 2 cups fresh basil leaves
> 4 medium-sized garlic cloves
> 1 cup walnuts or pine nuts
> 1 cup olive oil
> 1 cup freshly grated Parmesan cheese
> ¼ cup Romano cheese
> salt and pepper to taste
> 1 lb. pasta

Process the basil, garlic, and nuts in a food processor with a steel blade until finely chopped. With the machine running, pour in the oil in a thin steady stream. Add the cheese, a pinch of salt, and freshly ground pepper. Process briefly to combine. makes 2 cups—enough to cover 2 lb. of pasta.

Cook pasta according to package directions. Reserve a cup of water from the pasta. Add 1 cup pesto slowly to the pasta, stir until well-blended, and then add more sauce. Use pasta water to thin if mixture becomes too thick.

Add grilled salmon or chicken to make a full dinner entrée.

MAKES 8 SERVINGS

Spaghetti with Anchovies, Capers, and Olives

spaghetti alla puttanesca

In Naples, the "ladies of the night" make this pasta dish for themselves after returning home from a long night on the streets. We just think it is plain good anytime.

> ½ cup olive oil
> 1 teaspoon crushed red pepper
> 1 large clove garlic, minced
> 1 2-oz. tin of anchovies, drained and chopped
> 1 lb. ripe plum tomatoes, peeled, seeded, and chopped
> ½ cup capers, drained
> ½ cup oil-cured black olives, pitted and chopped
> ¼ cup sun-dried tomatoes in olive oil
> 1 lb. spaghetti

In a large skillet heat the olive oil over medium heat. Add red pepper and garlic, and cook until the garlic begins to color. Add the anchovies and swirl them in the oil until they begin to dissolve. Add the tomatoes, capers, and olives, and cook, covered, for 5 minutes.

While the sauce is cooking, purée the dried tomatoes with 1 tablespoon olive oil in a blender or food processor. Add to the sauce and continue to cook, covered, for 5 minutes. Turn the heat to very low to keep the sauce warm.

Cook the spaghetti in 6 quarts of salted water. Drain well and add to the sauce. Toss spaghetti in the sauce and turn onto a platter.

To peel tomatoes, drop them into a pot of boiling water for 2 minutes. Drain, cool, and slip off the skins.

MAKES 8 SERVINGS

Fettuccini Alfredo

This dish is easy to make and everyone loves it as a *primo piatto*. It goes well with veal and beef.

> 1 lb. fettuccini
> 1 stick butter
> ⅔ cup half and half
> 1 cup freshly grated Parmesan cheese
> ¼ cup freshly chopped parsley

Cook pasta in salted water. When pasta is tender but still firm, remove from water and drain. Reserve 1 cup of the pasta water.

Meanwhile, melt butter in a saucepan, then stir in the half and half and cheese. When warm, pour over the pasta. Toss with a fork until the pasta is well-coated and creamy. Sprinkle with the parsley and serve at once with more cheese and freshly grated black pepper.

MAKES 8 SERVINGS

Spaghetti with Eggs and Cream Sherry

spaghetti alla carbonara

My husband of thirty years introduced me to spaghetti alla carbonara when we were first dating. Any man who cooks should grab your attention. He won me over and continues to make it for us to enjoy. Bob uses pasturized eggs to make the sauce.

> 4 slices bacon, cut into 1 inch pieces
> 3 oz. proscuitto, chopped
> 1 medium onion, sliced
> ¼ cup cream sherry
> ½ cup butter, cut into pieces
> 1 lb. spaghetti
> 3 eggs, beaten
> ½ teaspoon salt
> freshly grounbd pepper
> 1 cup freshly grated Parmesan cheese

In a large pan sauté bacon. When almost crisp, add proscuitto and brown slightly. Drain bacon and proscuitto on paper towels.

Sauté onions in bacon drippings until soft. Return bacon and proscuitto to pan, stir in sherry, and simmer for 2 minutes. Remove from heat and add slices of butter.

Cook spaghetti in salted boiling water according to package directions. While spaghetti is cooking, beat the eggs in a bowl, add the salt and pepper, and set aside.

When pasta is cooked, drain and add to the pan with bacon, proscuitto, and onions. Pour the beaten eggs over the hot pasta mixture, and toss well. The heat of the pasta will cook the eggs.

Sprinkle with the cheese and serve immediately.

MAKES 8 SERVINGS

Linguine in Clam Sauce

linguine alla vongole

This recipe comes from the Bay of Naples. Whenever I prepare it, I think of the Amalfi Coast, the beautiful towns of Sorrento and Positano, and the Isle of Capri.

> 3 tablespoons olive oil
> 3 cloves garlic, minced
> 12 oz. can chopped clams, with liquid
> ½ cup shredded Parmesan cheese
> chopped parlsey
> 1 tablespoon pesto (optional)

Saute garlic in olive oil, but do not brown. Add clams with their liquid, and bring to a simmer. Cook pasta according to package directions. Drain. Pour sauce over pasta and toss. Sprinkle with cheese and parsley.

If desired, top with a tablespoon of pesto.

MAKES 8 SERVINGS

Pasta with Four Cheeses

pasta con quattro formaggi

I prepare this dish as part of my pasta class. My clients love it, and I hope you will too.

2 oz. Fontina, in strips
2 oz. Gorganzola, crumbled
2 oz. Provolone, in strips
½ cup freshly grated Parmesan cheese
½ cup heavy cream
1 lb. pasta

In a large pot bring 6 quarts of water to a boil. Salt the water. Add the pasta to the boiling water and cook until *al dente*.

Meanwhile, in a saucepan, combine Fontina, Gorganzola, and Provolone cheeses with the cream. Place over low heat and cook gently until cheeses have almost completely dissolved, about 5 minutes. Stir well and keep warm.

Drain the pasta and arrange it on a warm platter. Spoon the cheese sauce over the pasta, season to taste with salt and pepper, and toss well. Sprinkle the Parmesan over the top and serve.

Camembert, Brie, or Scamorza can be used in place of Fontina. Roquefort or Stilton can be used in place of the Gorganzola.

MAKES 8 SERVINGS

Pasta with Onion and Bacon

pasta con cipolle e pancetta

The porcini mushrooms help to intensify the flavors of this pasta.

⅓ cup dried porcini or
      6 oz. button mushrooms
6 tablespoons extra-virgin olive oil
10 oz. thinly sliced onions
½ cup white wine
3 oz. pancetta, cut into strips
1 lb. pasta, such as fusilli
salt
½ cup freshly grated Parmesan cheese

Place porcini in a bowl of warm water to cover and soak until softened, about 30 minutes. Drain, squeeze out any excess moisture, and chop finely. (If using fresh mushrooms, cut off and discard the stems, wipe clean with a towel, and slice.)

In a large frying pan heat 6 tablespoons of oil over medium heat. Add the pancetta and sauté, stirring occasionally, until golden, about 5 minutes. Add the onions, and sauté until translucent. Add the wine and mushrooms, and season with salt and pepper. (If using fresh mushrooms, add them with the onions.) Reduce heat and cover, simmering gently for 15 minutes.

Meanwhile cook the pasta according to package directions. Drain pasta and combine with sauce. Sprinkle with Parmesan cheese and serve.

MAKES 8 SERVINGS

Aromatic Sauce

salsa aromatica

The ingredients involved make this a classic Southern Italian dish. My friend Christina Pietro Sheran gave me the recipe. This sauce freezes well. It's delicious served before fish or veal.

2 cups Kalamata olives, pitted and halved
1½ cups olive oil
1 red and 1 yellow bell pepper, diced
1 red onion, diced
½ cup fresh lemon juice
3 cloves garlic, chopped
1 large bunch Italian parsley, chopped
1 large bunch basil, chopped
3 tablespoons anchovy paste
¾ cup capers
cracked red pepper to taste
1 lb. linguine

Saute onion, garlic, and peppers in olive oil until soft. Then add remaining ingredients and let simmer. Cook linguine in boiling water until al dente. Pour sauce over pasta and toss well.

MAKES 8 SERVINGS

Pasta with Tomatoes and Bacon

pasta all'amatriciana

This famous pasta dish comes from Rome. When we were children, our grandmother made it using the traditional long zitoni. We called them "little snakes." They would slide and slither all over our plates, which is why I suggest you use short ziti. Either way, this dish is so delicious it will make you famous too.

>   3 tablespoons extra-virgin olive oil
>   4 oz. pancetta, chopped
>   1 medium onion, chopped
>   1 28-oz. can diced tomatoes
>   ⅛ teaspoon hot red pepper flakes
>   ¼ teaspoon freshly ground black pepper
>   salt
>   1 lb. ziti, or tube-like pasta
>   1 cup grated Pecorino Romano or
>   Parmesan cheese

Heat oil in a 12-inch skillet. Add pancetta and onion, and cook for 5 minutes, or until both are soft. Remove from pan. Add the tomatoes; then add salt and red and black pepper. Cook for about 10 minutes, until the sauce is rich and thick.

Return pancetta to the pan, adjust the seasonings, cook another 5 minutes, then turn off the heat, and put cover on pan.

Cook pasta in boiling water until tender, stirring often. Drain pasta and add to the pot with the sauce, or add both to a large warm bowl. Toss well with the cheese and serve. Pass more cheese.

MAKES 8 SERVINGS

Pasta with Pesto and Salmon

pasta con pesto e salmone

Pesto is easy to make and delicious with salmon. I like to use grilled salmon on fettucini, though any long pasta works well.

>   ½ lb. cooked salmon, flaked
>   ½ lb. fettucine

Pesto Sauce:

>   8 oz. fresh spinach leaves
>   ½ cup fresh parsley
>   ½ cup grated Parmesan cheese
>   ¼ cup walnuts
>   1 garlic clove
>   1 tablespoon dried basil leaves
>   ½ teaspoon salt
>   ½ cup olive oil

Wash spinach leaves and parsley. Remove stems and chop in a food processor. Add remaining ingredients and process until smooth.

Cook and drain the fettucine. Toss pesto sauce and flaked salmon with hot fettucine, reserving a little salmon to sprinkle on top of each serving.

MAKES 4 SERVINGS

Carmela's Quick and Easy Pasta with Sausage and Peppers

pasta veloce con salsiccia e peperoni

We all need to take shortcuts at times. This recipe allows you to do just that, but no one but the cook will know you cheated.

¼ cup olive oil
1 large yellow onion, chopped
1 large yellow pepper, chopped
1 large red pepper, chopped
5 links mild Italian sausage
1 26-oz. jar Italian spaghetti sauce
1 lb. rigatoni or other tube-like pasta
¼ cup grated Parmesan cheese

Heat oil in a skillet. Chop onion and peppers and sauté them until they're slightly softened. Cut the sausage into 1-inch pieces and cook through. Add the jar of spaghetti sauce and bring to a boil. Let simmer for about 10 minutes.

Meanwhile, bring a large pot of water to a boil. Add pasta and cook according to package directions. Drain, reserving a cup of the water.

Add pasta to the sausage and pepper sauce. Toss well in the skillet. If the sauce seems too thick, add a little of the pasta water.

Add cheese and toss again.

MAKES 8 SERVINGS

Pasta with Mozzarella and Tomatoes

pasta alla caprese in crudo

This "no cook" sauce is easy to make anytime, but it tastes best during the summer, when the days are hot and the tomatoes and basil are at their most flavorful.

1 lb. ripe, juicy, cherry tomatoes
4 cloves garlic, peeled and finely chopped
10 fresh basil leaves, torn
½ lb. fresh mozzarella, cut into bite-sized pieces
pinch of red pepper flakes
1 teaspoon sea salt
freshly ground pepper
¼ cup exta-virgin olive oil
1 lb. penne or other pasta

Slice the tomatoes in half. Toss the tomatoes, mozzarella, garlic, basil, oil, sea salt, and red and black pepper in a large bowl. Leave to marinate for 30 minutes at room temperature.

Meanwhile, bring 6 quarts of water to a boil and cook the pasta according to package directions. Drain pasta, toss with sauce, and pass extra cheese.

Italians prefer their pasta "al dente," or "to the tooth." Check your pasta often while cooking to insure that it doesn't lose its firmness and become soft and mushy.

MAKES 8 SERVINGS

Potato Dumplings

gnocchi di patate

This heirloom recipe was handed down by my great aunt Elisa Tursi to my cousin Loretta Sieman. It is also served at my brother Bobby's restaurant, The Latin King, where it is one of the most ordered items.

2 lb. potatoes
2 egg yolks
1½ teaspoons salt
1½ cups flour
1 tablespoon melted butter

Use firm, dry potatoes. Scrub the potatoes and cook in boiling water until tender. Drain and peel.

Return potatoes to the saucepan and shake over low heat until dry. Mash the potatoes until they're very smooth.

Mix the egg yokes and salt. Add to the mashed potatoes. Add just enough of the flour to make dough. (This depends on the moisture in the potatoes.) Mix in the butter.

On a lightly-floured surface, roll the dough into finger-thick rolls. Cut into 1-inch lengths. Cook in boiling salted water until gnocchi rise to the surface. Remove with a slotted spoon.

Serve with melted butter and grated cheese, or with your favorite sauce.

MAKES 8 SERVINGS

Potato Dumplings
Daniella Ruggerio

gnocchi alla sorrentina

This recipe was given to me by Daniela Ruggerio. She uses only potatoes and flour in her recipe, because the potatoes provide enough mosture on their own. Daniella tops her gnocchi with a sauce from her Neapolitan roots.

Gnocchi di Patate:

2 medium white Russet potatoes
same volume-quantity flour

Boil or microwave the potatoes. They are cooked when the fork can be inserted easily. Peel and press or rice them. Once they're riced (not mashed) mix them to the same volume of flour. Even if the dough is still wet, use more flour only while shaping the dough into little balls.

Cook in boiling salted water for 7-9 minutes, or until gnocchi float to the surface. Taste one. When they reach your favorite consistency, drain.

Sauce:

1 28-oz. can diced or pureed tomatoes
5-6 fresh basil leaves
3 tablespoons olive oil
1½ teaspoons salt
1-2 teaspoons sugar
2 cups shredded mozzarella

Put first 5 ingredients together in a deep pot. Leave them to simmer for at least 15 minutes, or until sauce reaches the desired consistency.

Adjust salt to taste. Add to the drained gnocchi and top with the shredded mozzarella. (You can also bake everything in a 350° oven for 10-15 minutes.)

Gnocchi can be refrigerated in a single layer on a cookie sheet until ready to use. They can also be frozen in a single layer for 30 minutes and then transferred to a freezer bag. Use within three months.

MAKES 8 SERVINGS

Baked Rigatoni

pastachiena

Pasticcio is the word for things that are put together and then mixed up. That is what the recipe for *pastachiena* is like—pasta, meatballs, sauce, eggs, and cheese all mixed up in an oven-proof pasta dish and then baked until everything is bubbly and the cheese is nicely melted and stringy. This Calabrian dish was my favorite. My grandmother Carmela made it for special holidays.

Sauce:

> 1 lb. hot Italian sausage
> 1 garlic clove, minced
> ½ teaspoon oregano
> ½ teaspoon sweet basil
> ½ teaspoon parsley
> salt and pepper to taste
> 1 12-oz. can tomato paste
> 3 28-oz. cans tomato puree

Brown sausage. Add garlic and spices and simmer for a few minutes. Add tomato paste and tomato puree. Bring to a boil and simmer for two hours. If sauce becomes too thick, add some water. Add prepared meatballs (see next column), simmer one additional hour.

Meatballs:

> ½ lb. pork
> ½ lb. beef
> ¼ lb. Parmesan cheese
> 1 egg, beaten
> 1 teaspoon sweet basil
> 1 teaspoon fresh or dried parsley
> ½ cup chopped onion
> ½ cup dried breadcrumbs

Combine and mix all the ingredients. Roll into meatballs the size of marbles. Put on a cookie sheet lined with foil and bake for 10 minutes at 350°. When finished, add to the pasta sauce and cook for 1 hour.

Final assembly:

> 1 lb. mostaccioli, penne, or rigatoni
> ½ cup Parmesan cheese, grated
> 1 lb. mozzarella cheese, shredded
> 6 hardboiled eggs

Cook pasta slightly less than suggested on package.

In a deep oven-proof pasta dish add in this order: a layer of sauce and meatballs, a layer of cooked pasta, a layer of Parmesan and mozzarella cheese, more sauce with meatballs, a sprinkle of chopped egg. Repeat the layers a second time, reserving 2 sliced hardboiled eggs for the topping. Bake at 350° for 30 minutes or longer, until heated through.

Serve hot and bubbly.

MAKES 8–10 SERVINGS

Baked Lasagna

lasagna al forno

Lasagna is traditionally reserved for special occasions and events. The layering of pasta, meat sauce, and cheese make this the ultimate pasta dish.

2 lb. lean ground beef
2 12-oz. cans tomato sauce
1 6-oz. can tomato paste
2 teaspoons salt
1 garlic clove, minced
1 teaspoon ground red sweet pepper
1 teaspoon ground black pepper
¼ teaspoon oregano
½ teaspoon paprika
⅛-¼ teaspoon cayenne
½ teaspoon sweet basil
2 cups water
3 cups ricotta cheese or creamy cottage cheese
1 lb. lasagna noodles
1 lb. grated mozzarella
½ cup grated Parmesan cheese

Brown meat slowly. Add tomato sauce and tomato paste and cook for about 5 minutes. Add the next 8 ingredients. Simmer uncovered for 5 minutes, stirring. Then add 2 cups water, or more. Cook for 1½ to 2 hours on very low heat, stirring often.

Meanwhile, cook lasagne noodles in boiling water according to package directions. Drain, then pour cold water over the noodles.

Final assembly:

Using a large lasagna pan, 9 x 12 or larger, spread some of the meat mixture to cover the bottom of the pan. Lay half the noodles over this, pour some sauce over, spread the ricotta on the sauce, then the mozzarella. Repeat the layers, ending with the meat sauce. Top with grated Parmesan cheese. Bake in a 350°-375° oven for about 30 minutes. Remove from oven when hot and bubbly. Set aside for 10 minutes before cutting into squares.

This dish can easily be frozen. Remove from the freezer and defrost partially before baking.

MAKES 8 SERVINGS

73

Vegetable Lasagna

lasagna vegetariana

This recipe is very easy to make, yet it tastes like you've worked all day to prepare it. Italian Catholics often serve it on Friday nights during Lent.

2 cups sliced mushrooms
2 cups spinach leaves
1 cup chopped broccoli
1 cup chopped bell peppers
1 9-oz. package no-boil lasagna noodles
2 cups low-fat ricotta cheese
4 cups pasta sauce
1¼ cups shredded part-skim mozzarella
    cheese

In a medium bowl, combine mushrooms, spinach, broccoli, and bell peppers. Toss well. Lay ⅓ of the mixture in the bottom of a 9 x 13 inch baking pan coated with non-stick vegetable spray. Top with a layer of uncooked lasagna noodles, ⅓ of the ricotta cheese, and ⅓ of the sauce. Repeat layering until ingredients are used up, ending with pasta sauce. Sprinkle with mozzarella cheese. Cover with foil, and bake for one hour at 350°. Remove foil and bake 15 minutes longer or until lightly browned and bubbly.

This dish can be prepared ahead of time and refrigerated overnight before baking.

MAKES 10–12 SERVINGS

Sunday Spaghetti Sauce with Meatballs and Steak Rolls

spaghetti con polpette e braciole

Without fail this was our Sunday lunch while I was growing up in Des Moines. Mom would make the meatballs and steak rolls on Saturday, but would wait until after Mass on Sunday to brown them and make the sauce. We would eat promptly at 1 PM. My brothers Frank, Joey, and Bobby were often caught dipping a crusty piece of bread into the sauce, "Just to make sure it was safe for everyone to eat!"

Steak rolls:

> 8-10 small pieces of breakfast steak or very thin round steak, pounded ¼ inch thick
> olive oil
> ½ lb. bacon, diced
> 2 garlic cloves, chopped
> 4 tablespoons fresh parsley
> 4 tablespoons fresh basil
> salt and pepper

Mix bacon, garlic, parsley, basil, and seasonings together to make the filling. Lay small steaks on board or counter and sprinkle with salt and pepper. Spread 1-2 tablespoons of the filling on each steak, then roll it up, starting with the narrower end. Tuck in ends and secure with three toothpicks. Brown steak rolls in your favorite olive oil.

Meatballs:

> 1 lb. pork
> 1 lb. beef
> 4 eggs
> ¼ cup Parmesan cheese
> 1 garlic clove, minced
> 2 teaspoons salt
> 1 teaspoon pepper
> 2 teaspoons fresh parsley
> 4 slices bread, made into crumbs
> ½ cup water

Mix all ingredients together. Roll into balls. Brown well in olive oil. (These can be browned along with the steak rolls.)

Sauce:

> 3 tablespoons olive oil
> 2 12-oz. cans tomato paste
> 2 15-oz. cans tomato sauce
> 1 teaspoon Italian seasoning
> dash of crushed red pepper
> 4 cups water

Brown tomato paste in olive oil for 5-10 minutes; add tomato sauce, seasonings, and 4 cups water. Stir, heat, and simmer for 10 minutes. Put steak rolls and meatballs into the sauce and gently simmer for 2-3 hours, covered, stirring occasionally and adding water as necessary.

Serve with cooked pasta.

MAKES 8 SERVINGS

Manicotti

In the convents of Italy, you will see the "sisters" wearing manicotti (white cuff-like sleeves) to protect their black habits while working in the kitchen. I prefer to eat my manicotti, and you will too.

This recipe yields a light *crespelle* (crepe). Stuffed with the various fillings I have provided, you will have a delicious meal. In Italian families manicotti are reserved for special occasions. The original recipe is that of Gilda Pietro, who has lovingly handed down this recipe to her many daughters.

> 6 eggs
> 1 teaspoon salt
> 1½ cups cold water
> 1½ cups flour

Mix all ingredients with a mixer until smooth. Let the mixture rest in the refrigerator for 30 minutes. Ladle out batter into 4-inch circles on a hot, lightly-oiled griddle and cook until golden.

Fill each crepe with a generous tablespoon of filling (see following recipes) and roll up. They may be frozen at this point for up to a month.

If baking immediately, spoon pasta sauce over the manicotti and top with more mozzarella and Parmesan cheese. Bake at 350° for 30-40 minutes, or until nice and bubbly.

Filling I

> **3 lb. ricotta cheese**
> **8 oz. mozzarella cheese**
> **½ cup Romano or Parmesan cheese**
> **1 tablespoon freshly-chopped parsley**
> **salt and pepper to taste**
> **1 egg, beaten**

Mix first 4 ingredients together in a large bowl. Adjust seasoning, then add the egg and mix thoroughly.

Filling II

> **2 lb. ground beef**
> **1 lb. pork**
> **6 eggs**
> **6 slices of bread, made into crumbs**
> **½ cup Parmesan cheese**
> **1 lb. ricotta cheese**
> **salt and pepper to taste**
> **parsley and basil**

In a frying pan combine the meats and cook thoroughly. Drain and cool the meat. Add other ingredients and mix as you would for meatballs.

MAKES 8 SERVINGS

Sausage Manicotti

manicotti con salsicce

Manicotti:

> 3 beaten eggs
> 1 cup milk
> 1 tablespoon cooking oil
> 1 cup all purpose flour
> ½ teaspoon salt
> 2 tablespoons butter

Beat eggs, milk, and oil together. Gradually add the flour and salt. Beat until the batter is smooth.

Melt butter in a 6-inch skillet. Pour batter onto a hot pan and smooth out to make a thin crepe. Cook on one side, then turn and cook on the other side.

Filling:

> 2 lb. mild Italian sausage
> ½ cup chopped onion
> ½ cup mozzarella cheese
> 6 oz. ricotta cheese
> 1 teaspoon Italian seasoning
> salt and pepper

Cook sausage and onion together until the sausage is cooked through. Drain. When cooled add cheeses and seasonings.

Guido Fratini, Bob and Teddy Hobbins making pasta

Fill each crepe with 2-3 tablespoons of filling. Roll crepes and place them seam-side down on a greased baking dish. (Can be frozen at this point.)

Sauce:

> 4 cups pasta sauce
> ½ cup Parmesan cheese

Pour pasta sauce over crepes. Bake at 350° for 40 minutes. Sprinkle with Parmesan cheese and serve.

MAKES 8 SERVINGS

Secondi Piatti

Those of you who have never sopped up savory sauces with a slice of bread—shame on you! Let me tell you why.

I got this lesson in Italian table etiquette during Holy Week of 2002 when I had the privilege of making a Roman pilgrimage with my family. In an effort to have a more authentic Italian experience and to practice our *Italiano brutto* (language skills) we stayed with the Cinotti family—Flavia, Manuelo, and Paolo.

I was delighted to spend Good Friday with my brother crossing the city from one house of worship to another. Our first stop was Olympic Stadium, home of the Roman soccer team A. S. Roma, where we cheered the Italian goal makers. Our second stop was St. Peter's Basilica, home of the Pope. It was quite a unique experience hearing as many cheers and feeling as much fervor in church as in a stadium.

By the end of Holy Week, my family and I were exhausted from all the sightseeing, touring, worship, and socializing, and we were pleased when the Cinottis invited us to join them for their Easter lunch. They graciously shared their meal with us and also took pains to include us in the conversation despite the extra effort involved.

During the week, Paolo and Manuelo had introduced me to several customs and traditions—from saying *"piacere"* upon meeting someone new, shooting espressos to keep the day going, and singing the chants for the different soccer squads. At the Easter meal, I was taught one last lesson about the *scarpetta* or "little shoes." In the Italian tradition it is considered vulgar to use bread to soak up sauces. These pieces of bread are called "scarpetta"—the little shoes that are run through the sauces by uncouth diners.

At the meal, plate after plate of food passed by as my mouth watered. We started with antipasti -Maria's *Torta Rustica*—a tart made with ricotta cheese and mortadella, salami, and prosciutto. For the secondi piatti we had cannelloni filled with basil, fresh mozzarella and juicy sweet red tomatoes. The main dish was *Angello alla Cacciatore* or Hunter's Lamb. This delicious entree was done with basic ingredients—lamb, a few spices, garlic, onion, capers and local olives. Roasted potatoes, crisp asparagus, flavorful wines, limoncello (a digestivo and potent liquor), champagne, vin santo, and coffee complemented the meal.

Throughout the meal I was torn between anticipation and anxiety—excited for the feast but fearful that I would find it impossible to resist soaking up all the delicious sauce with a heel of bread.

I managed to make it through the meal using the correct forks and knives, toasting properly with wine, and saying please and thank you even as instinct encouraged me to curl over my plate and devour the food with my hands. It was the lamb that finally broke my resolve. Dripping with thin gravy, the roast was so tender, you barely had to chew it. As the meal passed and we were left with nothing but bones, sauces, and bread, I broke into a cold sweat as I contemplated the exquisite sauce on my plate. Just then, out of the corner of my eye, I saw Manuelo, Flavia's oldest and very sophisticated son, running a hunk of bread in laps around his plate. Was he raised by wolves? I nudged Manuelo and asked

Brian Hobbins and Manuelo Cinotti

in broken Italian, what about the "scarpetta"? He smiled at me as his mother tisk-tisked him. Turning to me she said, "Some rules were meant to be broken."

The moral of the story is this; the sauces that go over various dishes are like the frosting on a cake, they are meant to be enjoyed. I urge you to log many miles on your own *scarpettas* as you use the following recipes.

Italian Roast

manzo arrosto

This is a very simple and straightforward way to prepare a beef roast. In Italy they would most likely cook it on the stovetop. I like to roast the beef in the oven, freeing me to prepare other parts of the meal.

> 6 lb. rolled rump roast
> 2-3 garlic cloves
> 1 teaspoon sweet basil
> 1 teaspoon oregano
> 1 teaspoon salt
> 1 teaspoon lemon pepper
> ¼ cup fresh parsley
> 1 cup sliced yellow onion
> 1 cup sliced bell pepper
> ¼ cup olive oil
> 1-1½ cups dry red wine

Punch holes on top and bottom of roast at 2-inch intervals. Cut garlic into slivers and insert into holes. Mix the seasonings together and rub them into the roast. Set aside.

Sauté onion, bell pepper, and parsley in olive oil; then add roast and brown on all sides. Drain excess oil. Roast on a rack in a pan at 350° for an hour. Then add the dry red wine. Bake an additional hour, or longer if you prefer your meat well done. Baste the roast from time to time with the pan juices.

MAKES 12 SERVINGS

Sicilian Meatloaf

polpettone alla siciliana

The meat and cheese rolled into this meatloaf make an ordinary dish extraordinary. I love it hot as a *secondo piatto*, but its equally delicious the next day in a sandwich.

> 1½ lb. ground meatloaf mix (beef, pork, veal)
> 1 egg
> ¾ cup bread crumbs
> ½ cup finely chopped onion
> 1 teaspoon salt
> ½ teaspoon oregano
> ⅛ teaspoon black pepper
> 2 cups shredded mozzarella cheese
> 6 slices ham
> 2 cups spaghetti sauce

Combine ground meat, egg, bread crumbs, onion, spices, and ⅓ cup spaghetti sauce. Mix well and shape into a rectangle, about 10x12 inches, on a piece of waxed paper. Lay slices of ham over the top, overlapping the slices. Sprinkle the cheese over the ham. Roll up like a jellyroll and press ends to seal.

Place in a shallow baking dish. Bake at 350° for 1 hour. Drain off excess fat. Pour remaining sauce over meatloaf and bake an additional 15 minutes.

MAKES 8 SERVINGS

Stuffed Peppers

peperoni ripieni

My father, who is in his mid-eighties, still has a large vegetable garden that he maintains each summer. In mid-July the peppers, tomatoes and beans, along with many other vegetables, need to be harvested. That's when my mother's work really begins. When the peppers are ripe they must be fried, roasted, or stuffed. She will stuff a hundred peppers in one day and then send them off to her sons and friends to enjoy. She also will freeze the already-stuffed peppers to eat throughout the year. I'm not suggesting that you should plant a huge garden, as my father still insists on doing, nor that you should stuff a hundred peppers in a day. I am suggesting that you try her recipe for Peperoni Ripeini. I am sure that you and your family will enjoy them as much as we do.

1½ lb. ground beef
3 eggs, beaten
¾ cup breadcrumbs
parsley, basil and garlic to taste, chopped
salt and pepper to taste
2 cups of your favorite pasta sauce
6 to 8 peppers or a few more if your peppers
    are small

Sauté meat until it is no longer pink. Drain well. Add all of the remaining ingredients except peppers.

Wash the peppers, then slice off the tops and core them. Salt and pepper the inside and stuff with the meat mixture.

Grease a 9x13-baking pan and place the stuffed peppers in the pan. Pour pasta sauce over and between the peppers. Bake covered in a 350° oven for about 45 minutes. Uncover the pan and bake at 300° for an additional 15 minutes.

The peppers can be stuffed and then frozen for up to 3 months. Add pasta sauce when ready to bake. Pasta goes well with this dish; use the sauce from the peppers to dress your pasta.

MAKES 6–8 SERVINGS

Chicken Spiedini with Marinara Sauce

spiedini di pollo alla marinara

I make this dish with my young clients in my "Kids in the Cucina" classes. They love to make them, but they love to eat them even more. This recipe is an excellent way to get the young people in your life started in the kitchen.

> **2 lb. skinless, boneless chicken breasts (5 to 6)**
> **1 cup flour**
> **1 teaspoon kosher salt**
> **½ teaspoon pepper**
> **2 extra-large eggs**
> **½ cup grated Parmesan cheese**
> **1 cup seasoned bread crumbs**
> **olive oil**
> **unsalted butter**
> **bamboo skewers**

Lay the chicken breasts on a cutting board and slice each diagonally into 4 or 5 large strips.

Combine the flour, salt, and pepper on a dinner plate. Beat the eggs with 1 tablespoon of water on a second plate. Combine the Parmesan cheese and breadcrumbs on a third plate.

Dredge the chicken breasts on both sides with flour, then dip both sides into the egg. Roll in the breadcrumbs, pressing lightly to coat.

Heat 1 tablespoon butter and 1 tablespoon olive oil in a large sauté pan, and cook the chicken strips on medium-low heat for about 3 minutes per side or until just cooked through. Don't crowd the pan. Add more butter and oil and cook the remaining breasts. Serve each strip on a skewer, and dip in marinara sauce.

As an alternative, you can skewer the chicken, then dip in egg, flour, and bread crumb mixture. Brush with olive oil and butter, and bake in a 350° oven until cooked through.

MAKES 6 SERVINGS

Marinara Sauce

salsa marinara

> **3 tablespoons virgin olive oil**
> **1 large onion, finely chopped**
> **2 garlic cloves, chopped**
> **1 32-oz. can plum tomatoes**
> **1 32-oz. can tomato puree**
> **1 teaspoon salt**
> **6 basil leaves, chopped**

Warm the olive oil in a large skillet over medium heat. Add the onion and garlic. Cook, stirring often, until onion is translucent—3 to 5 minutes.

Stir in the tomatoes, tomato puree, salt, and basil. Cook for 20 minutes, stirring often.

MAKES 8 CUPS

Chicken with Prosciutto and Fontina

pollo con proscuitto e fontina

This dish is elegant enough to serve at a dinner party. It helps to flatten the breasts by pounding them with a mallet before rolling them into bundles.

2 tablespoons extra-virgin olive oil, plus extra
1 onion, diced
2 bay leaves
1 bunch escarole, cleaned and torn into pieces
8 boneless thighs or breasts, skin-on
8 slices Fontina cheese
8 thin slices proscuitto
salt and pepper

Preheat oven to 350°. In a large skillet over medium heat, warm the olive oil. Add the onion and bay leaves, and sauté until onion is translucent. Roughly tear the escarole, and add to the skillet. Sauté until the escarole just begins to wilt, and season with salt and pepper. Remove from the heat, and transfer to a baking dish.

On a clean work surface, arrange the chicken breasts skin side down. Pound with a meat mallet to flatten. Place a piece of Fontina on each breast, season with salt and pepper, and then top with a slice of proscuitto. Then roll each piece up tightly.

Place the chicken seam-side down on the escarole and drizzle with olive oil. Add salt and pepper and bake for 40 minutes.

MAKES 8 SERVINGS

Chicken Marsala

pollo al marsala

This pan-fried cutlet of crisp, golden-brown chicken is an Italian favorite, and the Marsala wine makes a divine sauce.

4 boneless chicken breasts
4 tablespoons flour
½ teaspoon salt
¼ teaspoon black pepper
2 tablespoons olive oil
2 tablespoons butter
1 - 1½ cups Marsala wine
¼ cup chopped parsley

Mix flour, salt, and pepper, and coat chicken well with the mixture.

Heat oil and butter in a heavy skillet until hot. Sauté chicken over medium heat until golden brown on both sides. Stir in the wine. Simmer, covered, until chicken is no longer pink, about 10 minutes. Remove chicken and keep warm.

Over medium-high heat, boil liquid in the skillet, scraping skillet to loosen brown particles, until liquid is reduced to about ½ cup. Pour sauce over chicken, and sprinkle with parsley before serving.

MAKES 4 SERVINGS

Chicken Cacciatore

pollo alla cacciatore

A classic Italian dish in the style of "the hunter."

1 2½-3 lb. chicken, cut into pieces
1 medium onion, sliced
2 garlic cloves, chopped
2 green peppers, cut into slices
2 cups sliced mushrooms
¼ cup olive oil
1 16-oz. can tomato sauce
1 8-oz. can chopped tomatoes
salt, pepper, and oregano to taste
½ cup dry white wine

In a heavy skillet, brown chicken in hot oil. When chicken is nicely browned and carmelized on all sides, remove from skillet. Cook vegetables in the same pan until they begin to soften. Then return chicken to the skillet. Combine tomato sauce, chopped tomatoes, and seasonings. Pour over the chicken and vegetables, cover, and simmer 30-40 minutes.

Stir in the wine. Cook an aditional 15 minutes uncovered. Skim off fat.

Serve with pasta and a good Italian bread.

MAKES 4 SERVINGS

Honey, Orange, and Rosemary Chicken with Linguine

pollo all'arancio e miele con linguine

The combination of honey, orange, and rosemary make this dish irresistible. The red pepper flakes spice it up.

3 ½ tablespoons honey
2 tablespoons plus 2 teaspoons orange juice,
    freshly squeezed
1¼ teaspoons rosemary leaves, crushed
⅛ teaspoon crushed red pepper
4 whole chicken breasts, halved
1 lb. linguine
¼ cup freshly-grated Parmesan cheese

Preheat oven to 350°. Combine all ingredients except chicken in a bowl. Dip the chicken breasts into the mixture and arrange in a shallow baking dish. Bake for 40-50 minutes, or until chicken is cooked throughout, using the remaining sauce to baste the chicken.

While chicken is baking, cook pasta according to package directions. Drain, reserving a cup of pasta water.

Remove chicken pieces from pan and keep warm. Add cooked pasta to the juices in the pan and toss well. If pasta seems dry, add some of the reserved water. Sprinkle with cheese, and top with the cooked chicken breasts.

MAKES 8 SERVINGS

Roasted Chicken

pollo arrosto

In Italy chickens roam about freely. When they come to the table they are plump and juicy. Purchase the plumpest chicken you can buy, preferably organic, for this elegant dish.

1 2½-3 lb. roasting chicken
1 tablespoon salt
1 teaspoon oregano
2 teaspoons paprika
2 teaspoons thyme
1 teaspoon freshly-ground black pepper
1 teaspoon garlic powder
1 large onion, chopped

In a small bowl combine salt, oregano, paprika, thyme, black pepper, and garlic powder. Set aside. Rinse and dry the chicken, then rub inside and out with the seasoning mixture. Place chicken in a sealed bag for 8 hours or overnight.

Remove chicken from the bag, add chopped onions to the cavity, and place in a roaster with a cover. Then roast, covered, for 1½-1¾ hours, in a 300° oven, until very tender and carmelized, basting chicken occasionally with the pan juices.

This recipe can easily be doubled, and two chickens can be roasted at the same time. Be sure to leave room around each chicken to allow them both to brown evenly.

MAKES 4 SERVINGS

Sage-stuffed Chicken Breast

pollo alla salvia

If you use a chicken breast with the skin on and meat still on the bone, the result will be a juicy flavorful chicken breast, unlike the dried-up, skinless, boneless ones to which we've become accustomed.

6 to 8 chicken breasts
sage leaves
salt and pepper
olive oil
Italian seasonings

Wash and dry the chicken breasts. Carefully lift the skin from the meat and salt and pepper the breast. Then stuff the sage leaves under the skin. Rub the outsides of the chicken pieces with olive oil, the Italian herbs, and more salt and pepper. Then bake for 1 hour at 350°, checking after 45 minutes. When nicely browned and when the juices run clear, the chicken is done.

MAKES 6–8 SERVINGS

Ricotta-stuffed Chicken Breasts

petti di pollo ripieni di ricotta

Marla and I served this endlessly during our catering days.

  2 medium onions, finely chopped
  2 tablespoons butter
  2 10-oz. packages frozen chopped spinach,
    thawed and squeezed dry
  2 lb. whole-milk ricotta
  2 eggs, beaten
  ¼ cup chopped parsley
  2 tablespoons fresh oregano or summer savory
  salt and freshly ground pepper
  nutmeg to taste
  16 halves of chicken breasts, boned, split, and
    skin on

Sauté the onions in butter until soft. Combine with the other ingredients except chicken. Mix well and season.

Trim excess fat from the chicken and place each breast skin-side up on a board. Loosen skin from 1 side of breast and stuff about ⅓ cup of the filling under the skin. Tuck the skin and meat under the breast, forming a round, even dome-shape. Put stuffed breasts in a buttered, Pyrex pan.

15 minutes before baking, preheat oven to 350°. Bake until golden brown—30-35 minutes.

Cut pieces in half and serve on a platter with fresh herbs.

MAKES 16 SERVINGS

Chicken Piccata

pollo in salsa piccata

The lightly-fried chicken cutlet marries well with the lemon sauce. Only fresh lemon juice should be used. This dish would go well with a nice herbed rice.

  4 boneless, skinless chicken breasts
  4 tablespoons flour
  ¼ teaspoon salt
  ¼ teaspoon black pepper
  2 tablespoons olive oil
  2 tablespoons butter
  ½ cup water
  6 tablespoons freshly-squeezed lemon juice
  ¼ cup chopped parsley

Mix the flour, salt, and pepper. Coat chicken well with flour mixture.

Heat oil and butter in a heavy skillet until hot. Sauté chicken over medium heat until golden brown on both sides. Stir in water and lemon juice. Simmer, covered, until chicken is no longer pink—about 10 minutes.

Remove chicken from the skillet and keep warm. Over medium-high heat, boil liquid in the skillet, scraping bottom to loosen brown particles, until liquid is reduced to about ½ cup.

Pour sauce over chicken and sprinkle with parsley before serving.

MAKES 4 SERVINGS

Baked Veal Parmesan

parmigiana di vitello al forno

When we were young my mother frequently served this dish for dinner. It's still one of our favorites.

⅓ cup bread crumbs
⅓ cup grated Parmesan cheese
salt and pepper to taste
1 egg beaten with 1 tablespoon water
4 veal cutlets (¼ inch thick)
1 8-oz. can tomato sauce
½ teaspooon oregano
⅛ teaspoon garlic salt
4 slices mozzarella cheese

Combine crumbs, cheese, salt, and pepper. Dip cutlets in egg mixture, then crumb mixture. Arrange in a baking dish and bake, uncovered, at 375° for 20 minutes.

Turn cutlets and bake for 15 minutes more.

Meanwhile, combine tomato sauce with ¼ cup water, oregano, and salt. Heat to a boil, reduce heat and simmer for 10 minutes.

Pour sauce over the meat. Top with the cheese slices. Return to oven. Serve when cheese is melted and sauce is bubbly.

MAKES 4 SERVINGS

Veal Involtini

involtini di vitello

I always enjoy eating veal because it's almost invariably tender. The addition of proscuitto and Fontina cheese makes this recipe even more delicious and festive.

6 veal cutlets
6 slices proscuitto
6 slices Fontina cheese
½ cup flour
1 tablespoon butter
1 tablespoon olive oil
1 cup dry wine
angel-hair pasta, cooked according
    to package directions

Place cutlets between 2 sheets of plastic-wrap and flatten to ⅛ inch. Wrap a slice of prosciutto around a strip of cheese and place in the center of a cutlet. Roll length-wise and secure with toothpicks. Sprinkle each roll with salt, pepper, and flour.

Heat butter and oil in a large skillet over medium-high heat. Add cutlets and sauté, turning frequently until well-browned. Remove from pan.

Add wine to the pan, bring to a boil, and reduce by half. Return cutlets to the pan, cover, and cook for 7 minutes more. Serve with angel-hair pasta.

MAKES 6 SERVINGS

Veal Cutlets

cotolette di vitello

After enjoying these veal cutlets at the home of John and Christina (Pietro) Sheran one Christmas, I begged them for the recipe, and they willingly complied. I'm sure you'll enjoy these golden cutlets too.

2 lb. veal cutlets
seasoned flour
Italian bread crumbs
egg wash—2 eggs, milk, and
    fresh parsley, chopped

Pound cutlets until very thin. Dredge in seasoned flour, then egg wash, and then the bread crumbs.

Fry cutlets until golden brown. Drain on paper towel. Lay in a single layer on a cookie sheet. Reheat in the oven just before serving, or eat at room temperature.

These cutlets can be made earlier in the day and reheated before serving.

MAKES 8 SERVINGS

Lamb Stew

agnello alla cacciatora

This lamb stew recipe is one of my favorite spring dishes. The carrots and snow peas make it very colorful. Just before serving top with some chopped parsley to make it seem even fresher. My version is cooked *alla cacciatore* or in the "style of the hunter." This dish is especially nice for Easter dinner.

4 tablespoons olive oil
3 lb. lamb, cut into 1- inch cubes
2 tablespoons flour
18 frozen pearl onions
¾ lb. snow peas
¼ cup balsamic vinegar
2 tablespoons tomato paste
2 cups rich beef stock (see soups)
    or prepared soup stock
1 cup dry red wine
1 medium onion, sliced
4 large carrots peeled and chopped in big
    chunks (or 16-20 cocktail-sized carrots)
5 garlic cloves, peeled and chopped
½ cup chopped parsley
1 teaspoon dried rosemary
1 teaspoon dried thyme
1 teaspoon sea salt
1 teaspoon freshly ground pepper
1 bay leaf

In a heavy skillet heat olive oil. Toss lamb with the 2 tablespoons flour. Over medium heat, brown the lamb, a few pieces at a time. Transfer to an ovenproof container or Dutch oven.

Rinse onions under cold water to thaw, set aside. Boil water. Trim and clean snow peas. When the water is boiling add snow peas for 1 minute. Plunge into a bowl of ice-cold water. Let cool and drain.

Preheat oven to 350°. When all the lamb is browned and in the Dutch oven, add vinegar, tomato paste, beef stock, and red wine. Stir well. Set Dutch oven over high heat and bring to a boil. Boil for 5 minutes. Add sliced onion, carrots, garlic, parsley, rosemary, thyme, salt, pepper, and bay leaf to the Dutch oven. Stir well and cover.

Bake for 1-½ hours; uncover for the last 15 minutes of baking. Toss in snow peas and pearl onions the last 15 minutes and serve garnished with chopped parsley.

Fresh herbs can be used and are readily available. Just double the amounts if you are going to use fresh. I like to serve this dish with very small pasta such as Rosa Marina or Orzo that has been tossed with olive oil. You can serve it on the side or put the pasta in the center of the plate, make a well and put the lamb and sauce over it.

A soft polenta would also be excellent.

MAKES 6 SERVINGS

Lamb Shanks

coscie di agnello

These lamb shanks make a comforting winter dish.

4 lamb shanks
¼-⅓ cup all-purpose flour
salt and freshly ground pepper
Dijon mustard to coat each shank
4 garlic cloves, crushed
2-3 cups dry red wine

Dust shanks with flour, salt lightly and pepper liberally. In a small bowl combine mustard and garlic, and mix thoroughly.

Coat the shanks with the mustard; then place them in a roasting pan. Roast at 400°, uncovered, for 15 minutes. Lower heat to 300° and add 2 cups of wine. Cover pan and roast 2½-3 hours, basting every 45 minutes. Add more wine or water if the pan becomes dry.

Serve when shanks have become tender and the meat is falling off the bone.

Serve lamb shanks with roasted vegetables such as potatoes, carrots, and leeks, and a robust red wine. This recipe can also be adapted for use with pork ribs, beef brisket, or chuck roast.

MAKES 4 SERVINGS

Grilled Lamb Chops

costolette di agnello alla griglia

Our family loves these easily grilled lamb chops. In the summer I prefer to grill them outdoors. They go well with roasted potatoes and grilled asparagus.

⅓ cup olive oil
juice of ½ lemon
2 garlic cloves, chopped
1 tablespoon dried rosemary
8 lamb chops
Lawry's Seasoning Mix
freshly ground pepper

Pour olive oil and lemon juice into a glass baking dish. Add chopped garlic, salt, and pepper to the mixture. Rub rosemary between the palms of your hands to release the flavor as you add it to the mixture. Finally, add lamb chops and turn them several times to coat thoroughly. Marinate for an hour. Grill or broil about 5-7 minutes per side. Serve when they are still pink in the center.

MAKES 4 SERVINGS

Herb-Rubbed Roast Pork

arista di maiale

When we prepare this roast as part of our culinary week at Il Mulino, the butcher has already seasoned the roast for us, and we cook it on the stove. At home I prepare the herbs myself and apply them on both the outside and the inside of the roast. Upon slicing the roast, you will see the beautiful stuffing in the center.

**1 cup mixed herb seasoning
    (parsley, rosemary, thyme, sage)
2 garlic cloves, minced
2 or 3 lb. boneless pork loin roast
olive oil
½ cup white wine
Lawry Seasoning Salt
fresh-ground black pepper**

Mix garlic with herbs; then rub on the roast to coat, while also stuffing some of the mixture inside the roast. (Do this early in the day or the day before if possible, to infuse roast with herbs.)

Heat oil in a pan and brown roast on all sides. Pour wine around the roast and put into the oven.

Roast at 350° until internal temperature is 160° (about 30-40 minutes per pound). Remove from oven and let stand for 10-15 minutes. Slice thinly and arrange on a platter. Pan juices may be poured over pork.

Use any combination of Italian herbs to equal at least one cup. Mix herbs with the seasoning salt and pepper; then apply to the roast.

MAKES 8 SERVINGS

Stuffed Squid

calimari ripieni

3 lb. squid, cleaned
2 cups dried bread crumbs
4 tablespoons olive oil
1 egg
1 tablespoon fresh parlsey, chopped
1 teaspoon oregano
¼ teaspoon salt
⅛ teaspoon black pepper
2 tablespoons water
2 onions, sliced
1 garlic clove, minced
1 tablespoon Romano cheese, grated
2-3 cups marinara sauce
angel-hair pasta, cooked

Clean squid. Hold the body in one hand and the head and tentacles in the other. Pull the tentacles away from the body. Cut off the head behind the eyes and discard. Squeeze the body to remove the cartilage. Rinse the tenacles and drain in a colandar.

To make the stuffing, mix together bread crumbs, 2 tablespoons olive oil, eggs, parsley, oregano, salt, pepper, cheese, and 2 tablespoons water, or enough to make the stuffing moist but not too soft. Add seasoning and cheese and mix well. Spoon stuffing into squid, leaving room for it to expand. Close each squid with a toothpick.

In 2 tablespoons of olive oil, brown the onions until golden. Pour marinara sauce into skillet, and place squid on top of the sauce. Cook on low heat for 30 minutes, making sure sauce continues to simmer. Adjust seasoning. Serve over cooked pasta such as angel hair.

MAKES 8 SERVINGS

Steamed Mussels

cozze al vino bianco

I love mussels anytime, as a *primi* or main course, hot or cold. Try making this recipe, it's simple yet elegant.

20 mussels, cleaned and beards removed
½ cup white wine
½ tablespoon garlic
6 oz. chicken stock
1½ tablespoons sun-dried tomatoes
1 tablespoon parsley
1 tablespoon basil
½ oz. garlic butter
½ oz. lemon butter

In a sauté pan, heat the mussels, white wine, and garlic. Add chicken stock, tomatoes, basil, parsley, garlic, garlic butter, and lemon butter, and bring to a simmer. Cover and cook over high heat until mussels open.

Place in a bowl and serve with crusty bread.

MAKES 4 SERVINGS

Shrimp with Tomato Basil Sauce

gamberi con basilico e pomodoro

The pasta cooks while you prepare the shrimp. Use already-prepared pasta sauce and this delicious dish comes together very quickly.

½ lb. penne pasta
1 tablespoon olive oil
1 cup onion, chopped
½ cup fresh basil leaves
1 tablespoon garlic, minced
1½ cups pasta sauce
½ cup heavy cream
1 lb. raw shrimp, peeled and deveined

Place penne in 2½ quarts boiling salted water, and cook until tender—about 10 minutes.

Heat oil in a pan over medium heat. Add chopped onion to the skillet and cook until soft.

Rinse basil, pat dry, remove stems, and chop.

When onions are soft, reduce heat to medium and add garlic, pasta sauce, and cream. Reduce heat to low and stir well. Add the shrimp and simmer, stirring freqently to turn the shrimp, for about 5 minutes, or until shrimp are opaque.

Add the chopped basil to the skillet and stir.

Drain the penne and place a portion on each serving plate. Top each serving with shrimp and sauce, and serve at once.

MAKES 4 SERVINGS

Scampi with Pasta

pasta con scampi

This classic seafood dish is a family favorite. Use the freshest shrimp you can find.

3 tablespoons butter
3 large garlic cloves, minced
1½ lb. fresh shrimp, shelled and deveined
¼ cup dry white wine
¼ cup tomato sauce
1¼ cups half and half
½ teaspoon basil
¼ teaspoon oregano
1 teaspoon salt
⅛ teaspoon pepper
1 lb. vermicelli or other long thin pasta
2 tablespoons finely minced parsley

Melt butter in a large skillet. Sauté garlic over medium heat, stirring, for 1 minute. Add shrimp and sauté over medium-high heat until the shrimp are bright pink on both sides, about 5 minutes. Add wine, tomato sauce, half and half, basil, oregano, and pepper. Heat through.

Cook pasta according to package directions. Arrange on a heated platter. Pour sauce over pasta. Sprinkle with parsley.

MAKES 6 SERVINGS

Mixed Fried Seafood

fritto misto di pesce

If you can't go to Via Reggio for the best Frito Misto in the world, then this is an excellent substitute.

vegetable oil for deep frying
1 cup unbleached all-purpose flour
fine sea salt to taste
3 lb. assorted firm fish fillets and shellfish,
    cut into uniform pieces
lemon wedges

In a deep fryer or large heavy pot, heat oil to 370°.

Mix flour and salt on a plate. Dredge the fish and shellfish in the flour, shaking off the excess, and fry in batches until golden brown. Remove from oil and drain on paper towels.

Place the fish and shellfish on a platter, sprinkle with salt, squeeze the lemon wedges over, and serve immediately with additonal lemon on the side.

Broiled Salmon

salmone gratinato

1 lb. salmon
2 teaspoons extra virgin olive oil
2 teaspoons fresh lemon juice
¼ teaspoon salt
pinch freshly ground pepper
2 garlic cloves, minced
2 teaspoons rosemary leaves, chopped,
    or 1 teaspoon dried dill

Cut fish into 4 equal portions. Combine the olive oil, lemon juice, salt, pepper, rosemary, and garlic in a bowl. Brush the mixture onto the fish and marinate for 15 minutes.

To broil, spray the rack of the pan with Pam or olive oil, and arrange the fish on top. Broil 4 inches from heat for 4-6 minutes per ½-inch of thickness. If the fish is more than 1 inch thick, turn halfway through broiling. When salmon flakes, it is done.

Always have fresh lemon wedges on hand to serve with this light dish.

MAKES 4 SERVINGS

Dried Cod Fish Marinara

baccala alla marinara

Baccala is a must for my family's Christmas Eve celebration, as part of the traditional Seven Fishes (see page 30). *Baccala* is salt cod and can be found in Italian specialty stores. It must be purchased several days ahead of serving because it needs to be soaked to remove all of the salt from the fish.

2 lb. dried codfish
2 tablespoons olive oil
½ medium onion, chopped
2 cups San Marzano tomatoes, crushed
½ cup chopped green olives
2 tablespoons capers
salt and pepper
1 tablespoon chopped fresh parsley and more
½ teaspoon dried oregano
lemon slices

Soak dried baccala in the refrigerator for 3 days, changing the water 3 times a day. Dry the baccala, cut into serving-sized pieces, and set aside. Heat the olive oil in a sauté pan, add the onion and sauté for 2 minutes. Add the tomatoes, chopped green olives, capers, parsley, salt, pepper, and oregano. Bring to a boil, and then add the *baccala*. Cook on the stove, or transfer to a baking dish and bake at 350° for 25-30 minutes, until the fish flakes when pierced with a fork. When ready to serve, sprinkle with more chopped parsley and lemon slices.

My mother. who is used to juggling many dishes at the same time, always makes her baccala in a sauté pan on the stove. If you are serving many different dishes, you may find it easier to begin the making of the baccala *on the stove and then finish it in the oven.*

MAKES 8 SERVINGS

Linguine Positano

My brother Bobby and sister-in-law Amy have a huge Christmas party annually for all of our aunts, uncles, and cousins. There are usually about a hundred of us at this event. We enjoy many dishes during the evening, but the centerpiece is Bobby's *Linguine Positano*. While the young adults are playing their dice games, the women are sipping their wine and cosmopolitans, and the children are running back and forth or playing with their new toys, the men of the Tursi family are in the basement kitchen preparing this fabulous dish one bowl at a time. As bowl after steaming bowl is handed out, we stop to enjoy the fresh seafood in the flavorful broth.

> 3 tablespoons olive oil
> ½ tablespoon fresh garlic
> 2 shrimp (12-15 count white shrimp, cleaned and deveined, butterflied with shell on)
> 3 little neck clams
> 3 oz. orange roughy (or any other white fish)
> 2 crab claws
> 1½ oz. lobster pieces
> salt and pepper
> ¼ cup white wine
> ¼ cup clam juice
> ½ cup fresh marinara sauce
> lemon
> 2 tablespoons basil leaves, shredded
> 1 tablespoon fresh Italian parsley
> crushed red pepper

Add olive oil to 10-inch sauté pan. Add ½ tablespoon of garlic and sauté until aromatic. Do not brown. Add the seafood as specified above and sauté, turning frequently. Add salt and pepper. Add white wine and clam juice. Cook down slightly. Add ½ cup fresh marinara and a squeeze of fresh lemon. Add torn basil leaves and parsley. Cook covered, checking from time to time. When clams are open the dish is finished. Do not overcook.

MAKES 1 SERVING

You can add crushed red pepper to make it spicy. You can also add one tablespoon of butter to make a smoother sauce. This may be served over linguine or as a zuppa di pesce.

My aunt, Darlene Tursi, my cousin, Pam Tursi, and my mother, Sarah Tursi, enjoying their Christmas Cosmos

Contorni

I grew up living next door to my paternal grandparents and within a few blocks of my mother's parents. Both sets of grandparents kept huge vegetable gardens and spent much of their time tending them. In addition to their vegetables, they also tended cherry, pear, apple, and apricot trees. I believe that planting the fruit trees and familiar vegetables was not only practical—it also allowed my family to bring a little bit of Calabria along with them to the United States.

As a young girl I often walked next door to find my grandfather picking tomatoes and my grandmother at the outdoor water spigot washing the lush red fruit she would shortly turn into tomato paste and sauce. She would call me over and speak to me in Italian about her days as a young girl. She told me stories of how she would climb the olive trees on her parents' land and shake the branches until the olives fell into the nets below; how they were collected, taken into town to the olive press and made into the liquid gold of olive oil. She spoke of the lemons and other fruits that grew on their trees and how she had to pick them carefully to avoid bruising them before her mother's inspection. Later I would help her carry the heavy pot of tomatoes to her basement kitchen where they would simmer all day, becoming the rich sauces we would enjoy throughout the year with our pastas and pizzas.

My grandparents, Frank and Carmela Tursi, my uncle Paul, and my father, Joe Tursi

Jars of tomato sauces and paste with beautiful basil leaves visible between the tomatoes and their glass walls were not the only treasures lining my grandmother's basement pantry. After the tomatoes came the fried peppers, the eggplant relishes, the beans and, of course, the beautifully canned jars of apples, cherries, pears, and apricots that we would find in our pies and desserts. Just to the side of these rows of canned fruits and vegetables was my grandfather's wine cellar. There, proudly, rested three oak barrels aging the wine that he had made using grapes from his garden vines.

I would be sent out to the garden to pluck some onions from the soil or to snip some oregano, parsley, and basil from the herbs so grandma could flavor the meatballs that we would be eating with our dinner. I would help my grandfather extract the seeds from his heirloom tomatoes and place them on pieces of white cotton cloth to dry on the windowsills of their home. Those seeds would be used to start the plants in the cold frame that he constructed for next year's crop.

Today, if l want to plant some tomatoes or herbs, I go to the farmers' market to buy well-established plants for my garden. I don't put up vegetables and fruit like my grandmothers did, nor do I know anyone who does. We just go to the giant supermarkets where many of these items can be purchased year-round, regardless of season or climate. But what I still have and use today, and what I share with you here, are the recipes carried by my grandmothers and my mother from that far away hill town of Terravecchia in Calabria.

Mixed Green Salad

insalta verde mista

Use only the freshest of field greens and best olive oil and balsamic vinegar when making this dish.

8 oz. mixed field greens
3 cups chopped fennel or celery
⅓ cup pine nuts
½ cup grated Parmesan cheese

Dressing:

¾ cup extra-virgin olive oil
¼ cup balsamic vinegar
salt and pepper to taste

Roast pine nuts for 5 minutes in a dry sauté pan. In a large bowl combine greens, fennel or celery, pine nuts, and cheese.

In a small bowl whisk together the dressing ingredients until dressing is emulsified. Pour the dressing over the greens and toss until well-coated. Serve on chilled plates.

MAKES 8 SERVINGS

Chicken Salad

insalata di pollo

I was first introduced to this lovely luncheon dish at Il Mulino on a recent culinary tour to Tuscany. We were spending the day at the 800-year-old farmhouse making tortelli with our instructor Anna Maria. Since we were preparing a large feast for our dinner, Maria's assistant, Daniela, prepared this chicken salad for our lunch. I now serve it to my own guests when entertaining and demonstrate how to make it as part of my classes. It's perfect for a light weekend lunch.

4 skinless boneless chicken breasts
Lawry's Seasoning Salt
pepper
dried Italian herbs
olive oil
1 package of organic field greens or spring mix
½ cup toasted pine nuts
½ cup Parmesan cheese

Salad dressing:

¾ cup olive oil
¼ cup balsamic vinegar
salt and pepper to taste

Wash and dry the chicken. Season the breasts with Lawry's Seasoning Salt, pepper, and dried Italian herbs. Drizzle with olive oil. Bake in a preheated 350° oven for 30 minutes or until cooked completely through. Remove from oven and cool.

Meanwhile, put all the ingredients for the dressing into a bowl and whisk until they are emulsified.

When chicken has cooled, cut the breasts into slices. Toss the salad greens with the dressing and arrange on a large flat plate. Place the chicken on top of the salad, and sprinkle with pine nuts and Parmesan cheese.

To take this dish one step further, cut some tomatoes and hard boiled eggs into wedges and arrange around the outside of the plate. Make sure to drizzle with additional olive oil and to sprinkle on some sea salt and pepper.

MAKES 12 SERVINGS

Escarole Salad with Pine Nuts

insalata di scarole con pinoli

Escarole is used frequently in Italian cuisine, but we do not use it very much in our cooking. I encourage you to try this leafy green vegetable. I think you'll like it.

¼ lb. escarole (1 bunch)
2 tablespoons pine nuts
2 tablespoons olive oil
2 tablespoons fresh lemon juice
salt and pepper to taste
2 tablespoons fresh parsley, minced

Tear escarole into bite-sized pieces, wash, and spin dry. Transfer to a heat-proof bowl.

In a small skillet, cook the pine nuts in the oil over medium heat, stirring, until they are golden. Working quickly, transfer the pine nuts with a slotted spoon to the escarole. Stir the escarole and then drizzle with the hot oil from the pan, tossing well. Drizzle the lemon juice and toss well.

Sprinkle with salt, pepper, and parsley, and serve.

MAKES 4 SERVINGS

Beans and Pasta

pasta fagioli

My grandmothers made this for their husbands because it was both nutritious and inexpensive.

1 lb. dried white beans
6 cups water
2 tablespoons salt
1 15-oz. can chopped tomatoes or tomato sauce
1 garlic clove
1 carrot, chopped
1 teaspoon salt
½ cup Parmesan cheese
½ cup chopped celery
¼ teaspoon ground black pepper
1 onion, chopped
1-2 small potatoes, chopped
½ pound small pasta
4 tablespoons olive oil

Cover beans with water and soak overnight. Drain beans and cover with 6 cups fresh water along with 2 tablespoons salt. Bring to a boil and simmer for 1 hour.

Add all the other ingredients except pasta, oil, and cheese, and simmer for another hour.

Meanwhile, cook pasta according to package directions and drain. Before serving, add pasta to the bean mixture. Ladle into pasta bowls. Drizzle with olive oil, sprinkle with Parmesan cheese, and serve.

MAKES 8 SERVINGS

Tuscan Bean Salad

insalata toscana di cannellini

The people of Tuscany are known as *mangia fagioli* or "bean eaters." You will often find a bean salad on the menu or at the table when dining there. This simple recipe uses canned beans rather than dried, so the long hours of soaking the beans are avoided, although the result is equally delicious. Try this bean salad with the Sage Stuffed Chicken Breasts. Or make the salad, then mash the beans lightly and spread on crostini. Drizzle with olive oil and you have an easy antipasto.

2 15-oz. cans cannellini beans
    (great northern beans can also be used)
1 tomato, seeded and diced
¼ cup red onion, chopped
2 tablespoons freshly squeezed lemon juice
I teaspoon freshly chopped thyme leaves
    (sage leaves could be substituted)
½ teaspoon kosher salt
¼ cup olive oil

Rinse the beans in a colander and drain. Chop the tomato, onion, and thyme. Add the beans. Mix with the lemon juice, salt and olive oil. Toss well. Refrigerate for several hours before serving so the flavors will blend.

MAKES 8 SERVINGS

Roasted Garlic

aglio arrostito

Mashed cloves of roasted garlic can be mixed with warmed olive oil or melted butter and spread on bread, tossed with pasta, or stirred into whipped potatoes or rice.

5-6 large heads garlic
2 tablespoons olive oil
coarse salt
freshly ground pepper

Preheat oven to 350°. Cut off tops of garlic and loosen. Place each head of garlic on a piece of aluminum foil, drizzle with olive oil, and sprinkle with salt and pepper. Wrap each piece of foil into a tight package, place on a cookie sheet, and roast for 1 hour.

Remove from the oven. When cool enough to handle, remove the garlic by squeezing each clove at one end until it pops out of its skin.

Mash the garlic and spread on crusty bread.

MAKES ½–1 CUP

Zucchini Sticks

bastoncini di zucchini

These zucchini sticks can also be served as an antipasto. They can be made ahead and reheated.

8 small zucchini
extra-virgin olive oil
Parmesan cheese
salt and pepper

Cut zucchini in half length-wise, then quarter. Dip sticks in the olive oil. Then dip and roll in Parmesan cheese. Broil until toasty brown, turn, and toast other side.

MAKES 32 SERVINGS

Grilled Zucchini

zucchini alla griglia

I make grilled zucchini often in the summer when there is an abundance of it. I especially like to use mint with this dish.

4 or 5 medium zucchini, both yellow and green
2 tablespoons olive oil, plus more for the grill
2 teaspoons balsamic vinegar
1-2 teaspoons mint, finely chopped, or
    ¾ teaspoons dried oregano
salt and pepper to taste

Wash zucchini and cut into ¼ inch slices. Mix olive oil, balsamic vinegar, herbs, salt and pepper,

and pour mixture over zucchini, making sure both sides are well-coated. Set aside for at least an hour.

Brush grill with olive oil. Place zucchini on grill, and grill for 3 minutes on each side. After turning, brush with left-over olive oil and vinegar mixture.

Place slices of zucchini on a platter, with slices overlapping. Adjust seasonings.

Eggplant can be substituted for zucchini.

MAKES 8 SERVINGS

Stuffed Zucchini

zucchini ripieni

This recipe is a good way to make use of the large zucchini that we seem to have so much of in the summer.

1 large zucchini
1 lb. ground beef
1 lb. ground chuck
1 garlic clove, minced
3 eggs
1 cup bread crumbs
½ cup grated Parmesan cheese
salt and pepper
spaghetti sauce
¾ cup shredded mozzarella cheese

Split a large zucchini in half lengthwise. Cut into sections. Scoop out and discard the seeds. Scoop out the flesh, leaving a ¼-inch shell. Dice the scooped-out flesh.

Brown meats together with minced garlic. Drain and add diced zucchini, eggs, bread crumbs, grated Parmesan cheese, salt, and pepper. Mix well.

Stuff mixture into zucchini shell. Grease a pan with olive oil. Place the zucchini in the pan and bake for 15 minutes at 350°, covered. Then cover with the spaghetti sauce and bake another 45 minutes. Sprinkle mozzarella over the top and bake until cheese melts.

Remove from oven, set aside for 5 minutes. Cut into serving pieces.

MAKES 8 SERVINGS

Zucchini Pancakes

frittele di zucchini

My grandmothers always made this dish using the vegetables they harvested from their large gardens. They always served them with a little pasta sauce. I prefer to eat them with sour cream.

4 cups zucchini, coarsely grated
salt
4 eggs, separated
1 cup Parmesan cheese
½ cup minced green onion
⅓ cup flour
¾ teaspoon dried mint
salt and pepper
1 tablespoon butter
½ cup sour cream

Put grated zucchini in a colander. Salt lightly and let stand for 15 minutes. Rinse and squeeze out excess water.

In a large bowl combine egg yolks, cheese, green onion, flour, mint, and salt and pepper to taste. Add grated zucchini.

In a separate bowl, beat egg whites until they form soft peaks. Fold into zucchini mixture.

Melt butter in a skillet over medium heat. Spoon ¼-cup portions of zucchini mixture into skillet and fry on both sides until golden and crisp.

Serve topped with sour cream.

MAKES 8 SERVINGS

Sautéed Summer Vegetables

peperonata

When Bob and I are in town on summer weekends we rise very early and make a trip to the Minneapolis Farmer's Market to hunt out the freshest and ripest of summer fruits and vegetables. I love to go from stall to stall and grower to grower picking out the produce I will cook for my family later in the day. After a visit to the market you can be sure this recipe for *peperonata* will be on our family table.

3 tablespoons olive oil
1 large eggplant, cut into quarters lengthwise
 and then into ½ inch cubes
2 large onions, peeled, halved, and thinly sliced
2 yellow peppers and 1 red pepper, cored,
 seeded, and cut into strips
4 medium ripe tomatoes cut into 1 inch chunks
3-4 zucchini, both green and yellow, sliced
⅔ cup fresh-chopped basil
salt and pepper to taste

Pour olive oil into a large pan or pot. Add eggplant, onion, and bell pepper. Cook over medium heat, stirring and shaking pan, for 8 minutes, or until vegetables start to soften. Add tomatoes and zucchini. Simmer for another 15 minutes, or until vegetables are tender. Add basil and season with salt and pepper.

MAKES 12 SERVINGS

Roasted Potatoes

potati arrostiti

Easy to make, these potatoes are requested by my sons whenever they are at home. I prefer to use red potatoes for this recipe.

2 lb. potatoes
salt and pepper
Italian herbs
olive oil

Wash potatoes and cut unto small wedges. Place in a roasting pan in a single layer. Toss well with salt, pepper, and Italian herbs. Coat with olive oil and toss again, making sure that the each wedge is well-seasoned.

Place potatoes in the oven and roast at 350° for 50-60 minutes, or until they are golden brown and crunchy.

MAKES 8 SERVINGS

Grilled Vegetables

verdure grigliate

1 eggplant
1 zucchini
1 summer squash
1 red and 1 yellow bell pepper
1 8-oz. package whole mushrooms
1 red onion

Marinade

¾ cups olive oil
¼ cup balsamic vinegar
1 garlic clove, chopped
1 tablespoon Italian seasoning
salt and pepper to taste

Chop vegetables. Mix marinade ingredients together. Combine vegetables and marinate in a large ziplock bag for several hours or overnight.

In a grill-pan over medium-high heat grill vegetables until they are tender yet still crisp. Vegetables can also be roasted in a single layer in an oven at 450° for 10-15 minutes.

These vegetables look beautiful on a white platter. Garnish with parsley. Baby cut carrots also make a nice addition. Parboil them for 5 minutes before adding to the marinade.

MAKES 8 SERVINGS

Stuffed Tomatoes

pomodori ripini

4 firm medium tomatoes
salt and pepper
3 slices French bread
handful fresh parsley
1 garlic clove
handful chopped basil
¼ cup Parmesan cheese
¼ cup olive oil

Cut tomatoes in half. Discard seeds, sprinkle with salt, invert on paper towels, and drain for 30 minutes.

Grind bread into fine crumbs in a food processor or blender. Finely chop parsley. Mince garlic. Combine crumbs, parsley, basil, garlic, and cheese. Add a dash of black pepper. Add oil slowly until crumbs moisten. Stuff the tomatoes with the bread mixture. Bake in a pre-heated 350° oven for 10 minutes.

MAKES 8 SERVINGS

Marinated Zucchini

zucchini alla marinara

Another great recipe for using up our summer zucchini.

3-4 medium-sized zucchini, cut into rounds
⅔ cup olive oil
¾ cup Italian parsley
⅛ teaspoon pepper
2 garlic cloves, crushed
¼ cup basil
salt to taste

Place all the ingredients in a large ziplock bag, and marinate for 2-4 hours. Drain the zucchini and grill for about 5 minutes on each side. This can be done on an outdoor grill, on a grilling pan indoors, or in the oven.

This marinade also works well with eggplant.

MAKES 8 SERVINGS

Fried Eggplant

melanzana fritte

This recipe can be made ahead and reheated just before serving. It is also excellent as part of an antipasto platter.

1 eggplant
eggwash
seasoned Italian bread crumbs
oil (canola)

Cut eggplant into rounds and then cut each round in half. Salt and drain. Make an eggwash of egg, milk, salt, and pepper. Dip each piece of eggplant in the wash, then in the breadcrumbs. Fry in hot oil until brown.

Drain on paper towels. Lay on a cookie sheet and place in a warm oven until ready to serve.

MAKES 4 SERVINGS

Eggplant with Ricotta

menza luna

Menza luna can be served as a vegetarian meal or as a side to meat or fish.

1 eggplant
salt and pepper
basil
garlic
Romano cheese
1 lb. ricotta cheese
parsley
2 eggs, beaten
flour
olive oil
proscuitto
spaghetti sauce

Slice eggplant into rounds, salt, and drain on paper towels to eliminate the bitterness. Mix together basil, garlic, Romano cheese, ricotta cheese, parsley, salt and pepper. Dip dried eggplant first in egg, then flour. Sauté in the olive oil. Drain slices on paper towels.

On a greased cookie sheet, lay out half of the eggplant and top with a scoop of the ricotta mixture. Lay slices of proscuitto over the ricotta and top with more slices of eggplant. Cover with your favorite spaghetti sauce. Sprinkle more Parmesan cheese over the top and bake at 350° for 30 minutes, uncovered.

When bubbly and heated through, remove from the oven. Let stand for 5 minutes before serving. Garnish with sprigs of basil.

MAKES 4 SERVINGS

Asparagus Spears with Proscuitto

asparagi proscuitto

Asparagus, proscuitto, and Parmesan cheese are a wonderful combination. These little bundles are easy to make, but delicious.

asparagus
Italian salad dressing
proscuitto
Parmesan cheese

Blanch several bunches of asparagus—at least 40 spears. Marinate overnight in your favorite Italian salad dressing.

Drain asparagus. Gather together in bundles of five, and wrap a slice of proscuitto around each bundle. Lay bundles in a lightly-oiled 9 x 13 pan. Sprinkle Parmesan cheese over the bundles. Bake at 350° until heated through—about 10 minutes.

MAKES 8 SERVINGS

Orange and Red Onion Salad

insalata di arance e cipolle

This salad is both colorful and very fresh-tasting. I make it in one of my classes in Sicilian cooking, and everyone who tries it loves it.

4 navel oranges
2 red onions, sliced very thin and
    separated into rings
1 head curly lettuce

Dressing

2 tablespoons reserved orange juice
2 tablespoons white wine vinegar
1 small garlic clove, minced
½ teaspoon ground cumin
salt and pepper to taste
½ cup olive oil

Working over a bowl to catch the juice, cut away the peel of the orange. Reserve juice. Slice oranges crosswise and chill, covered, on a large platter for at least 15 minutes, and up to 4 hours.

Let onion rings soak in ice-water for 30 minutes to 1 hour. Drain and pat dry.

In a blender or bowl, blend 2 tablespoons orange juice, vinegar, garlic, cumin, salt and pepper. Add oil in a slow steady stream, blending to emulsify.

Arrange cleaned lettuce around the perimeter of a large platter. Spread orange slices, overlapping the lettuce. Place onion rings on top of oranges. Drizzle the dressing over the oranges and onions and decorate with more lettuce.

Chopped black olives make a nice addition to this salad.

MAKES 4 SERVINGS

Tomato and Mozzarella Salad

insalata caprese

2½ lb. roma tomatoes
⅓ cup extra virgin olive oil
½ lb. fresh mozzarella cheese
2 tablespoons fresh basil
½ teaspoon kosher salt
½ teaspoon coarse black pepper

Remove the stems from the tomato and core. Slice vertically from top to bottom into ¼-inch slices. Cube mozzarella. Toss with the oil, salt, pepper, and basil.

Spread some field greens on a platter, then place tomato slices on top. Add cheese mixture.

Cherry or grape tomatoes could be used instead of roma tomatoes. Instead of the mozzarella, try a small package of garlic and herb feta cheese.

MAKES 8 SERVINGS

Tomato, Pepper, and Onion Salad

insalata di pomodori, peperoni e cipolle

This salad is best made in the late summer when the tomatoes are at their juiciest. Have plenty of crusty Italian bread on hand to sop up the flavorful juices. When we were growing up my mother made this salad almost every night in the summertime.

4 tomatoes, chopped
4 bell peppers, cut into wedges
1 red onion, coarsely chopped

salt and pepper to taste
4 tablespoons olive oil
several leaves fresh basil
½ teaspoon dried oregano, or
more if using fresh

Mix all of the ingredients together. Let marinate at room temperature for 1 hour before serving.

MAKES 8 SERVINGS

Tomatoes Stuffed with Vermicelli Pesto

pomodori ripieni al pesto

These stuffed tomatoes look beautiful on a platter surrounded by fresh greens.

12 medium tomatoes
1½ lb. vermicelli
½ cup pesto
basil leaves

Pesto

½ cup pine nuts
4 garlic cloves, peeled
1 teaspoon kosher salt
½ teaspoon ground pepper
3-4 cups fresh basil leaves
¼ lb. Parmesan cheese, grated
¼ lb. Romano cheese, grated
1½-2 cups olive oil

Process the pesto ingredients in a food processor until smooth. Cut tomatoes in half with a sharp serrated knife, then remove the seeds and membranes using a melon ball scooper. Turn the tomatoes upside-down on a rack to drain.

Cook the vermicelli in a large kettle of boiling salted water. Drain well. Mix pasta and pesto together in a bowl. Let cool to room temperature.

Fill each tomato with some of the pesto mixture and top each with a basil leaf before serving.

MAKES 24 SERVINGS

Olive Salad

insalata di olive

As a young girl I always looked forward to occasions when my mother would make this salad. It should be served well-chilled.

4 5-oz. jars pimento-stuffed olives
1 red onion, chopped
2 jars marinated artichoke hearts, chopped
heart of celery, chopped
1 teaspoon oregano
1 package Good Seasonings salad dressing,
    made according to package directions
oregano

Chop olives, onion, and celery hearts. Add oregano to the salad dressing, and pour dressing over mixture. Marinate for several hours. Pour into a glass bowl or lettuce-lined platter.

MAKES 8 SERVINGS

Italian-style Spaghetti Squash

spaghetti di zucca

Spaghetti squash is fun to prepare and serve, and good for you too. It is an excellent substitute for pasta.

2 lb. spaghetti squash, halved lengthwise
    and seeded
¼ cup butter
20 sage leaves
grated Parmesan cheese (optional)
freshly grated black pepper

Place the squash halves, cut side down, in a baking dish. Add ¼ cup water and cover with foil. Bake at 350° for 1 hour, or cover with plastic wrap and microwave on high for 8 to 10 minutes until tender. Cool slightly.

Melt butter in a pan and sauté the sage leaves. Using a fork, scrape the squash strands into a bowl. When the butter is golden add the squash strands and toss well. Add some grated Parmesan cheese and freshly ground black pepper. Toss until well-coated.

MAKES 8 SERVINGS

Our wedding reception was held at the Val-Air ballroom in West Des Moines, Iowa. Because I was the only daughter in my family, several hundred guests were invited. We all ate a large dinner, and then the real fun began. In keeping with tradition, Bob and I had the first dance, while my aunts and cousins showered us with Jordan almonds and other Italian candies, as well as coins to ensure our good fortune and wealth. Then our parents, the rest of the bridal party, and the other guests joined us on the dance floor.

The party grew livelier still when, after several hours of romantic and pop tunes, the band turned to polkas and tarentellas which everyone at the wedding, young and old alike, danced together. Finally we took up the Grand March, that intricate dance that requires at least four directors to organize. Several hundred of us marched around the ballroom a few times with a partner, then again in groups of four, and again with eight. Somehow the directors eventually assembled us into a bridge and each one of us passed under it single file.

The reward for all of this marching and hard work was the wedding cake and cookies. Bob and I were the first to finish the dance, and we were immediately directed to the wedding cake that stood proudly, five layers high, flanked on either side by banquet tables covered with the many different wedding cookies that my mother and her friends had been making by the bushel basket for days. We cut the cake, enjoyed a taste, and then had a champagne toast. Only then were our guests allowed to get to the tables with the cookies.

As Bob and I left for our honeymoon that night, we turned to watch our friends piling their plates with a selection of the many different treats available. As is the custom in our family, at the end of the reception each guest was invited to take home an additional plate of cookies to enjoy the next day and to remember the wedding by.

You may never have to put on such an extravagant event as this, and I am happy that I won't have to either. Even in Italian families today, many of the customs have been cut back. Not many of those wonderful women are alive anymore. Their daughters are now married and many are grandmothers. No one talks about making a bushel of *Crustli*, *Guantas* or Love Knots anymore, but they still often will make a batch of one of their favorites for their family to enjoy, and so I hope that you will too.

Pizzelles with Raspberry Sauce

pizzelle con salsa di lamponi

This is a beautiful dessert and frequently served at the Carnevale in Venice.

1¾ cups flour
2 teaspoons baking powder
salt
3 eggs
¾ cup sugar
1 stick butter
1 teaspoon vanilla extract

To serve

2 tablespoons sugar
1 cup raspberries
1 cup heavy cream whipped into peaks
    with 2 teaspoons sugar
1 pint fresh raspberries

In a heavy bowl sift together the flour, baking powder, and a pinch of salt. In a separate bowl whisk the eggs and sugar until smooth. Add the melted butter and vanilla, and whisk to combine. Add the flour mixture, a little at a time, until it is all incorporated.

Heat a pizzelle iron and coat the surface with cooking spray. Add about 1 tablespoon of the batter and close the lid. Cook for 30 seconds, or until golden, and remove to wire racks to cool and harden. Repeat with the remaining batter, cutting six of the pizzelles in half before they turn crisp.

Meanwhile, place the raspberries in a blender and add 2 tablespoons of sugar. Purée until smooth, adding water if necessary. Strain the sauce.

Lay 1 whole pizzele on each of 6 plates. Add a dollop of whipped cream and stand a pizzele-half on top, using the whipped cream to anchor it.

Spoon some raspberries around and finish with the raspberry purée.

Pizzelles can be made ahead and frozen for up to a month, or kept in an air-tight container for several days.

MAKES 12 SERVINGS

Emma Fattor's Apple Cake

torta di mela

This delicious apple cake recipe was given to me by my friend Lynn Matte Gibbs, who had gotten it from her maternal grandmother, Emma Guiliani Fattor, from Castelfondo, Italy. I first started making this recipe when I was in college and still make it today. It is one of our favorite fall recipes and after you have sampled it I am sure it will become one of your fall staples as well.

8 apples, peeled and diced
2 cups of sugar
2 teaspoons cinnamon
2 eggs
½ cup of butter or margarine
1 teaspoon vanilla extract
½ cup chopped walnuts
1 cup raisins
1 teaspoon salt
2 to 2½ cups flour
2 teaspoons soda

Mix the first 3 ingredients together. Blend together the eggs, butter, vanilla, walnuts, raisins, and salt; add to apple mixture and let stand for 30 minutes. Then add the entire mixture to the flour and soda and mix all together.

Put into 2 well greased 9x5 loaf pans and bake at 350° for about 60 minutes.

Serve warm with vanilla or cinnamon ice cream.

MAKES 2 LOAVES

Grazietta's Schiacciata Fiorentina

I was introduced to this light cake when I attended cooking school in Italy. I love the fact that you use tablespoons as measurements. Fresh berries go nicely with the cake.

7 tablespoons sugar
2 eggs
7 tablespoons milk
7 tablespoons olive oil
9 tablespoons flour
1 tablespoon baking powder
juice and peel of one orange
peel of one lemon
fresh fruit such as strawberries,
**   blueberries, or raspberries**

Mix everything together and pour into a greased, round 9-inch pan. Bake at 350° for 30 minutes, checking often. Let cool and dust with powdered sugar before serving. Slice and top with fruit.

MAKES 8 SERVINGS

Elisa Tursi at 75

Cream Puffs with Raspberries

zepolle beigne ai lamponi

My great aunt, Elisa Tursi, made *zepolle* to celebrate the feast of St. Joseph on March 19th every year. She always deep-fried her puffs, which were delicious. Over the years I have found that most of my clients want to stay clear of fried foods, so I now bake my cream puffs, but find them equally delicious.

1 cup water
½ cup butter or margarine
1 cup sifted flour
4 eggs

Heat oven to 400°. Bring water and butter to a boil. Remove from heat and stir in all of the flour. Beat vigorously with a spoon until thoroughly blended. Stir over heat 1-3 minutes until mixture comes away from the pan to form a ball. Remove from heat and beat in eggs one at a time. After each addition, beat until batter is well-blended and smooth.

Drop dough by rounded teaspoons onto ungreased baking sheets and bake for 25-30 minutes. Cool puffs, cut in half, and fill with desired filling.

Almond Cream Filling

creme alle mandorle

1 package instant French vanilla pudding
1 teaspoon almond extract
1 pint whipping cream
1 pint raspberries
powdered sugar for dusting

Follow direction on package of vanilla pudding, substituting almond extract for some of the milk. Let pudding set for 1 hour. Whip the cream until stiff peaks form. Fold whipped cream into the pudding.

Slice cream puffs in half and fill with the almond cream. Top with some raspberries. Put top back on the puff and dust with powdered sugar. Garnish with a raspberry.

MAKES 12 SERVINGS

The Latin King Restaurant, Des Moines, Iowa

Latin King Cannoli

My youngest brother, Bobby, bought the Latin King restaurant, a Des Moines landmark, more than twenty years ago. The previous owner was our cousin, Jimmy Pigneri. Over the years we have held many family celebrations there, including my parents' wedding luncheon and my wedding shower. The restaurant has been renovated several times, and so has the recipe for Cannoli. My sister-in-law Amy has substituted cream cheese for some of the ricotta, which results in both a firmer and a smoother consistency.

> 2 8-oz. packages cream cheese, at
>   room temperature
> ½ cup ricotta cheese
> 2 tablespoons sour cream
> 6 tablespoons heavy cream
> 1 tablespoon sugar

1 tablespoon freshly-squeezed lemon juice
grated lemon zest to garnish
3½ oz. powdered sugar
1 oz. semi-sweet chocolate, chopped
1 teaspoon vanilla extract
cannoli shells

Blend all ingredients except shells in a food processor until very smooth. Stuff the cannoli shells with the mixture. Refrigerate until ready to serve. Garnish with lemon zest.

This recipe makes about 2¾ cups of filling. It can be refrigerated for a week.

MAKES 10–12 SERVINGS

My father, Joe Tursi, and my brother, Bobby Tursi

Zia Melina's Cannoli

Zia Melina made excellent cannoli, and she made them often so everyone could enjoy them.

Filling

>   2 lb. ricotta
>   1½ cups sugar
>   5 oz. chocolate, chopped
>   2 teaspoons cocoa
>   powdered sugar

Pastry

>   3 cups flour
>   ½ cup sugar
>   1 teaspoon salt
>   3 tablespoons Crisco
>   2 tablespoons wine
>   2 tablespoons water
>   1 egg
>   oil for frying

Mix filling ingredients together and refrigerate.

Mix the ingredients for the pastry together and refrigerate for 30 minutes. Roll out pastry as thinly as possible, cut into squares, and roll around cannoli forms.

Heat oil to 350°. Drop cannoli carefully into the oil. Fry until golden brown and then drain on paper towels. When cool, stuff with filling and dust with powdered sugar. Keep refrigerated.

MAKES 12 SERVINGS

Almond Jam Tart

crostata di marmellata e mandorle

This recipe is not only delicious but easy to make.

>   1½ sticks butter
>   ⅓ cup sugar
>   ½ teaspoon almond extract
>   1½ cups all-purpose flour
>   1 cup jam or preserves (raspberry, blueberry, strawberry, or apricot)
>   ½ cup sliced almonds

In an electric mixer, beat butter and sugar together for 4 or 5 minutes, or until pale and fluffy. Reduce speed to low and add almond extract, followed by flour. Mix until combined. Reserve ½ cup of the dough, cover with plastic wrap and chill.

Press remaining dough into a 10 x 1 inch tart pan with removable bottom. Chill until firm, about 30 minutes, or as long as overnight.

Preheat oven to 350°. Remove tart pan from refrigerator and spread jam over the crust. Remove reserved ½ cup of dough from refrigerator and crumble over the jam. Sprinkle evenly with almonds.

Bake in the middle of the lower oven rack until the crust is golden, 30-40 minutes. Cool on a rack. Remove tart pan's side, and serve at room temperature or warm, with whipped cream or ice cream if desired.

Rhubarb sauce substitutes nicely for the jam.

MAKES 12 SERVINGS

Amaretto Cheesecake

crostata di formaggio amaretti

I love Amaretto, so this cheesecake is one that I really enjoy.

1-2 tablespoons butter, at room temperature
¾ cup Amaretto cookie crumbs
2 lb. cream cheese, at room temperature
¼ cup fresh lemon juice
2 tablespoons Amaretto
1 teaspoon vanilla extract
1½ cups sugar
4 eggs at room temperature

Heat oven to 325°. Coat bottom and sides of springform pan with butter; then cover with the crumbs and refrigerate while preparing batter.

Beat cream cheese at medium speed until smooth. Continue beating while adding lemon juice, Amaretto, and vanilla, until smooth. Add sugar slowly. Add eggs 1 at a time. Remove pan from refrigerator, and pour batter into pan.

Set into a larger pan holding 1 inch of hot water. Bake for 75 minutes, until set and lightly brown.

Take both pans out of the oven. Leave together for 20 minutes. Then remove cheesecake pan, and let set for 4-5 hours. Refrigerate.

This cheesecake can be made in a 9-inch springform pan or a 9x5x3 loaf pan.

MAKES 12 SERVINGS

Cream Cheese Cupcakes

dolcetti di crema formaggio

These mini-cheesecakes were one of the most popular items on the Occasions Catering menu. Make ahead and freeze them; then top with fresh fruit or pie filling a few hours before serving. They are especially nice when entertaining large groups.

3 8-oz. packages cream cheese
1 cup sugar
1 cup sour cream
¼ cup sugar
5 eggs
1½ teaspoons vanilla
fresh fruit, preserves, or pie filling

Cream together cream cheese and 1 cup sugar. Add eggs 1 at a time, beating after each addition. Add vanilla.

Divide mixture into 24 cupcake liners in cupcake pans. Bake 40 minutes at 300°, until lightly browned.

Meanwhile, mix together sour cream and ¼ cup sugar. Spread 1 teaspoon of the mixture on each cupcake. Bake 5 minutes more. Let cool and refrigerate. Before serving top with fruit.

Cupcakes can be frozen. When ready to use, just thaw and top with fresh fruit or fruit pie filling.

MAKES 24 SERVINGS

Hazelnut Cheesecake

crostata di formaggio e nocciole

Cheesecake is always a nice way to end a meal, although you won't find them made in Italy.

Crust

    1½ cups finely ground vanilla wafers
    ¾ cup hazelnuts, shelled, toasted, and ground
    2 tablespoons sugar
    2 tablespoons butter, melted

Filling

    3 8-oz. packages cream cheese,
        at room temperature
    1 cup sugar
    3 eggs, lightly beaten
    3 tablespoons Frangelico (hazelnut liqueur)

Topping

    1 pint sour cream
    2 tablespoons sugar

Combine vanilla wafer crumbs, nuts, sugar, and butter. Pat mixture into the bottom of an 8-inch springform pan. Refrigerate until firm, about 30 minutes.

Preheat oven to 300°. Bake crust 15 minutes. Let cool completely.

Increase oven temperature to 350°. Beat cream cheese at low spead in large bowl. Gradually add 1 cup sugar. Add eggs and liqueur and blend until completely smooth. Pour into cooled crust and bake until set, about 45-50 minutes. Let cool slightly.

For the topping, combine sour cream and remaining sugar. Spread mixture over cheesecake to within ½ inch of the edge. Bake 5 minutes.

Preheat broiler. Watching carefully, run cheesecake under broiler until top is lightly browned, about 1-2 minutes. Let cool.

Refrigerate at least 5 hours, or overnight.

MAKES 12 SERVINGS

Italian Cream Cake

torta glassata

This recipe was given to me by my aunt, Darlene Tursi. I like to make this cake in the spring, and even for an Easter dessert.

An assortment of tortes from our cooking class

Cake

- 5 eggs, separated
- 2 cups sugar
- 1 stick butter
- ½ cup shortening
- 1 teaspoon vanilla extract
- 2 cups flour
- 1 cup buttermilk
- 1 teaspoon soda
- 1 cup angel-flake coconut
- 1 cup chopped nuts

Frosting

- 1 8-oz. package cream cheese
- 1 stick softened butter
- 1 lb. powdered sugar
- 1 teaspoon vanilla extract
- 1 cup chopped nuts

Beat egg whites until stiff and set aside. Cream sugar, butter, shortening, and vanilla. Add egg yolks one at a time. Add the remaining ingredients except egg whites. When everything is mixed together gently, fold in the egg whites.

Line 3 round 9-inch cake pans with parchment paper and spray with Pam. Spread mixture evenly between the pans. Bake at 350° for about 25 minutes, until a toothpick inserted in the middle of the cake comes out clean.

For the frosting, cream together cream cheese and butter. Add powdered sugar and vanilla. Add the nuts last. Frost the 3 layers. Then assemble into a 3-layer cake.

MAKES 12 SERVINGS

Tiramisu

Tiramisu literally means "pick me up" in Italian. This classic version will surely give you a lift.

3 pasteurized eggs, separated
½ cup sugar
1 to 2 teaspoons instant espresso powder
    according to taste
2 tablespoons brandy or cognac
1 lb. Mascarpone cheese
20 lady fingers, toasted in oven for 5 minutes
1 cup brewed espresso
cocoa powder to sprinkle

Combine 3 egg yolks, sugar, espresso powder, and cognac. Beat well for 2-3 minutes. Add the cheese and beat another 5 minutes. Beat the 3 egg whites with a little sugar until stiff. Fold into the cheese mixture until blended.

Brush lady fingers with the brewed espresso (be careful not to soak too much.) Layer the lady fingers with the cheese mixture, then repeat the layering, ending with the cheese. Sprinkle with more cognac if you want more liquor flavor.

Sprinkle with cocoa powder. Chill for at least 4 hours, and preferably overnight.

Decorate with maraschino cherries if desired.

You can make this in a 13 x 9 inch pan, or layer in a large glass bowl. Doubles easily. For a different flavor use Bailey's Irish Cream liqueur in place of the cognac.

MAKES 12 SERVINGS

Fruit Salad

macedonia

When visiting my relatives in Rome recently, I noticed that all of my female cousins ordered fruit for dessert, rather than a heavy torta or a scoop of gelato. They told me that the fresh fruit dessert satisfied them as much as something much higher in calories. This is a really nice dessert to have anytime, using whatever fruits are in season.

juice of 3 large sweet oranges
juice of 1 lemon
1 banana
1-2 apples
1-2 pears
2 peaches
5 apricots
1 cup green grapes
1 cup berries
any other fruits that are in season
2-3 tablespoons sparkling white wine

Juice the oranges and lemon. Slice the banana; core and slice apples and pears. Remove the pits from the peaches and apricots and slice. Remove the grapes from their stems. Add all fruit including the berries in a glass bowl. Pour juice and sparkling wine over the fruit. Toss gently. Cover the bowl and refrigerate for at least 2 to 3 hours.

This can be served with vanilla ice cream or whipped cream.

MAKES 12 SERVINGS

Italian Trifle

zuppa inglese

This popular Italian dessert is known as English soup, but really has little to do with England. I have been making this easy version of *zuppa inglese* for years, and it is one of my family's favorites. Using a purchased pound cake, angel food cake, or ladyfingers, this recipe is so easy that a child could make it, yet so festive that it's suitable for any special occasion you might be celebrating.

> 1 large frozen pound cake, angel food cake,
>   or 2 packages of ladyfingers
> 1 -3 oz. package instant French vanilla pudding
> 1 pint of whipped cream
> 4 tablespoons Amaretto liqueur
> 1 cup of raspberry preserves
> 1 3-oz. package sliced almonds
> Maraschino cherries

Cut the pound cake or angel food cake into cubes. (Leave the ladyfingers whole.) Prepare the pudding according to package directions and refrigerate for 30 minutes. Whip the cream until it forms soft peaks. Refrigerate until ready to assemble.

To assemble, place half of the cake in a trifle or clear glass bowl and sprinkle with half of the Amaretto. Spread ½ cup of the raspberry preserves over the cake, allowing some to dribble down the sides. Pour ½ of the pudding over the preserves. Spread ½ of the whipped cream over the pudding.

Repeat the layers ending with the whipped cream. Sprinkle the almonds over the whipped cream and decorate with Maraschino cherries. Refrigerate for 2 to 3 hours before serving.

When ready to serve, scoop the *zuppa inglese* into a bowl and top with a cherry.

MAKES 12 SERVINGS

Peaches With Amaretti Stuffing

pesche ripieni

Make this luscious dessert in the summer when the peaches are at their best. Serve the peaches hot with vanilla ice cream for the perfect ending to a meal, or cold the next day. (This recipe can easily be doubled.)

4 ripe peaches without blemishes or bruises
juice of ½ lemon
⅔ cup of crushed Amaretti cookies
    (these can he purchased in Italian
    specialty stores)
2 tablespoons Amaretto liquor
2 tablespoons butter at room temperature,
    plus 1 more tablespoon to coat the
    bottom of the baking pan
½ teaspoon vanilla extract
1 egg yolk

Preheat the oven to 350°. Wash peaches and cut in half. Remove the pit of the peach and enlarge the hole slightly to hold the filling.

Sprinkle the peaches with the lemon juice. Crush the cookies to make ⅔ cup. Soften the crumbs in the Amaretto for 10 minutes.

Beat the butter until soft and add it to the Amaretti mixture along with the other ingredients. Mix well.

Divide the mixture into 8 parts and stuff the peaches, packing the stuffing down lightly. Then arrange them in a baking pan that has been lightly buttered. Bake for 35-40 minutes. Remove from oven and let cool slightly. Serve with vanilla ice cream.

MAKES 4 SERVINGS

Fresh Apricot Tart

crostata de albicocche fresche

Make this wonderful tart in May and June when apricots are in season.

Almond Pastry

 1¼ cups flour
 ¼ cup almonds, blanched and ground
 ¼ cup sugar
 ½ cup butter
 1 egg yolk
 ¼ teaspoon vanilla extract
 ¼ teaspoon almond extract

Fruit Topping

 4 cups apricots (about 2 lb.) halved and pitted
 ⅓ cup sugar
 1 teaspoon cornstarch
 ⅛ teaspoon ground nutmeg
 2 tablespoons butter
 ⅔ cup apricot preserves
 1 tablespoon orange-flavored liqueur
 ¼ cup toasted, sliced, almonds

To make the pastry, mix flour with ground almonds and ¼ cup sugar. Cut in ½ cup butter until pastry mix is crumbly.

Blend egg yolk with vanilla and almond extracts. With a fork, stir egg mixture lightly into flour mixture. Then, using your hand, press dough into a smooth flat ball. Wrap well and chill for 30 minutes.

Preheat oven to 450°. Using hands, press chilled pastry into bottom and up the sides of a round, 11-inch, removable-bottom tart pan.

Arrange apricots, cut side down and slightly overlapping, in the pastry-lined pan. Mix together sugar, cornstarch, and nutmeg, and sprinkle over apricots. Dot with 2 tablespoons butter.

Bake for 12 minutes at 450°. Reduce heat to 350° and bake until apricots are tender and crust is brown. (25-30 minutes.) Cool in pan on a wire rack.

Heat the apricot preserves until melted and bubbly. Strain out solid pieces of fruit; discard solids. Add liqueur. Brush mixture over apricots. Lightly sprinkle toasted sliced almonds around perimeter of tart.

Remove pan sides. Serve tart at room temperature.

MAKES 12 SERVINGS

Grandma Lattan's Italian Pound Cake

torta margherita

My friend Norma Muldowney learned how to make this cake by watching her mother, who never bothered to measure things. "Just some of this and a little of that," she would say. Here Norma shares the results of her investigations with us.

> 6 eggs (yolks and whites separated)
> 3 cups flour
> 3 teaspoons baking powder
> 2½ cups sugar
> l cup oil
> l cup milk
> 1 lemon (the entire rind grated and
>   all of the juice)
> 3 teaspoons cream of tartar

Preheat oven to 350°. Grease an angel food cake pan. Separate the egg whites and beat the 6 yolks with 2½ cups of sugar until thick. Beat in the milk and oil, a little at a time. Stir in the 3 cups of flour and the 3 teaspoons baking powder. Add the lemon rind and the juice.

In another bowl, beat the egg whites with the cream of tartar until stiff. Fold the egg whites into the yolk mixture. Pour into prepared pan, and bake at 350° for about 75 minutes, or until tester comes out clean. Let cake cool and remove from pan. Dust with powdered sugar.

MAKES 16 SERVINGS

Crème de Menthe Squares

dolci di cioccalato con crema di menta

The marriage of mint and chocolate in this recipe creates a wonderful bar.

> 1½ cups butter, divided
> ½ cup unsweetened cocoa
> 3½ cups powdered sugar, divided
> 1 egg, beaten
> 1 teaspoon vanilla extract
> 2 cups graham crackers
> ⅓ cup green crème de menthe
> 1½ cups chocolate chips

For the bottom layer, combine ½ cup of the butter and cocoa powder in a saucepan. Heat and stir until well-blended. Remove from heat. Add ½ cup powdered sugar, egg, and vanilla. Stir in graham cracker crumbs. Mix well and press into the bottom of an ungreased 9 x 13 inch pan.

For the middle layer, melt another ½ cup butter, and combine with crème de menthe in a small mixing bowl at low speed. Add the remaining 3 cups powdered sugar while mixing at low speed until smooth. Spread over chocolate layer. Chill 1 hour.

For the top layer, combine the remaining ½ cup butter and chocolate chips in a small saucepan. Cook and stir over low heat until melted. Spread over chilled mint layer, return to refrigerator and chill 1-2 hours. Cut into small squares and serve.

MAKES ABOUT 4 DOZEN

Amaretto Butter Cookies

biscotti di amaretti

I love making these cookies because the dough is so easy to work with and the end result so pretty. Serve them with a cup of tea or coffee for a nice mid-afternoon snack.

1 cup butter at room temperature
1 cup sugar
1 large egg, separated
3 tablespoons Amaretto liqueur
2 teaspoons orange peel
2 cups all-purpose flour
¼ teaspoon salt
1¼ cup sliced almonds

In a large bowl, with mixer on medium speed, beat 1 cup of butter and sugar until smooth. Add egg yolk, liqueur, and orange peel, and beat until well blended.

In another bowl mix flour, baking powder, and salt. Add to the butter mixture, stir to mix, and then beat until blended. Gather dough into a ball, divide in half, and flatten each portion into a disk. Wrap tightly in plastic wrap and freeze until firm enough to roll without sticking, about 30 minutes.

Unwrap dough. On a lightly floured surface, with a floured rolling pin, roll out the disk to about a ¼-inch thickness. With a floured 2-inch round cookie-cutter, cut out the cookies. Place about 2 inches apart on a buttered 12x15 inch baking sheet. Gather excess dough into a ball, re-roll, and cut out remaining cookies.

In a small bowl, beat egg white with 1 teaspoon of water to blend. Brush cookies with mixture and sprinkle or arrange ½ teaspoon sliced almonds on each.

Bake cookies at 325° until lightly browned, about 15 minutes. Let cookies cool about 5 minutes before removing. Use a wide spatula to remove them from the baking sheet.

I like to arrange 5 sliced almonds like spokes on top of each cookie.

MAKES ABOUT 4 DOZEN

Thumb Print Cookies

biscotti con marmellata

This cookie is both beautiful and delicious. Try using several different jams or preserves to give them added variety.

1 cup soft butter
1 teaspoon vanilla extract
½ cup packed brown sugar
2 eggs, separated
2 cups flour
½ teaspoon salt
1½ cups finely chopped walnuts or pecans

Mix butter, vanilla, brown sugar, and egg yolks in a bowl. Add flour and salt. Roll into balls the size of walnuts.

Beat egg white slightly. Dip balls into whites and roll in chopped nuts. Bake at 350° on greased cookie sheet for about 10 minutes. Press thumb gently on top of each cookie, and fill with preserves. Then bake an additional 5 minutes.

MAKES 4-5 DOZEN

Filled Cookies

biscotti cini

My grandmother Carmela Tursi taught my mother, Sarah, how to make these unusual cookies. I love all Italian cookies, but these are my favorites. Just ask my husband Bob. We always leave one in the jar, both of us waiting for the other to enjoy it. I watch that lonely cookie for a week before I cave in and devour it. I guess Bob has more willpower than I do. Make these for your family and they will love you.

Filling

1 lb. nuts, chopped
1 lb. raisins
zest of one orange or
       3 oz. orange marmalade
2 teaspoons (or less) cinnamon
1 18-oz. jar grape jam
2 teaspoons whiskey

Dough:

1 cup butter
1½ cups sugar
6 eggs
1 teaspoon vanilla
4 cups flour
4 teaspoons baking powder
½ teaspoon salt
½ cup milk

To make the filling, cook the raisins, jam, and orange zest (or marmalade) together until jam starts to thicken. Let cool; then add cinnamon, nuts, and whiskey and mix together again. Cover, and let set in refrigerator overnight.

To make the cookies, mix butter, sugar, eggs, and vanilla together. Add flour, salt, baking powder, and milk. Mix well. You may need to add more flour, so that the dough can be rolled out like a pie crust.

Roll out dough and cut into 2½-inch squares. Put 2 teaspoons of the filling on each square, fold over, and seal the edges with a fork. Snip top with scissors to vent, then bake at 350° until light brown, 12-15 minutes. When cooled, frost or sprinkle with powdered sugar.

(As an alternative, roll out the dough into a long 10x4 inch rectangle. Spread filling down center and fold crust over filling. Roll into a log, seam side down. Tuck ends under and snip top with a scissors to vent. Then bake at 350° for about 15-20 minutes, until lightly browned. When done, they will look like logs. Let them cool.)

Meanwhile, to make frosting, mix together 1lb. powdered sugar, ½-¾ stick butter, 1-2 table-spoons milk, and 1 teaspoon lemon extract, until it reaches a spreadable consistency. Spread frosting by hand on top of the logs. Let frosting dry; then cut the cookies on the diagonal into 1-inch slices.

MAKES ABOUT 10 DOZEN

Tardilla or Struffoli

My grandmother, Carmela Tursi, and her sister-in-law, my great aunt Melina Tursi, made these often. As a child I could not wait for them to come out of the deep fryer. I would pop them immediately into my mouth, although they were even better coated with honey or cut into diamond-shapes and decorated with sprinkles.

The *Tardilla*, (as the Calabrese call them) or *Strufoli* (as they are called in other regions of Italy) can also be mounded on a pretty platter, then sprinkled with candy. To eat just pull apart with two forks.

12 eggs
1 teaspoon salt
1 teaspoon baking soda
7 cups flour
1 lb. jar honey

Beat eggs with salt, then add soda and flour, a cup at a time. Mix with a spoon at first, and then with your hands, adding more flour at the end if the dough is too soft.

Roll a piece of dough into a long rope. Cut the rope into ¼-inch pieces that look like beads, and spread them on floured boards or cookie sheets until ready to fry.

Fry in hot oil (360°) a few at a time. When they are nicely browned, remove and drain in a colander, or pat dry with paper towels.

When cooled, heat the honey in a large pan for 10 minutes. Add tardilla to the honey in small batches, coating them well, and being careful not to burn yourself. Then spoon them out onto a buttered breadboard or pan. With damp hands, pack beads closely together.

Put in refrigerator for 3 hours or overnight. Then cut into squares, rectangles, or diamond-shapes by cutting diagonally. Store them in a cool place after they have been cut or they will soften and fall apart. Decorate with sprinkles after they have been cut.

MAKES 6–8 DOZEN

Italian Wedding Cookies

guantis

For years, my mother and her friends would gather together to make bushel-baskets of *guantis* for their children's weddings. Each lady had her own special job to do. One would mix the dough, another would knead it, one would roll out the pastry, still another would form the shapes, and so on. When the cookies were finally done, they were lovingly packed in bushel baskets with waxed paper between the layers to protect the crisp, delicate cookies. On the day of the wedding my mother and her friends would take out their best silver platters, line them with white doilies, and gently pile the trays with the lovely pastries.

I will never forget the sight of all those darling Italian women gathered together, scarves wrapped around their heads, talking, telling stories, giving orders to one another, and laughing all the while. What a bond they had to their families and to one another!

1 dozen large eggs
½ stick softened butter
1 teaspoon vanilla
1 teaspoon baking powder
¼ cup sugar
6 cups flour

Beat eggs in a deep bowl. Add remaining ingredients to make a soft but not sticky dough. Knead well and let the dough rest for about 5 minutes.

Place dough in a bowl and keep covered. Roll out a small amount of dough at a time. (A pasta machine can be used.) Roll each piece as thin as possible. Cut into narrow strips about 4 inches long. Form into shapes such as bowties, wreathes, or braid three strips together.

Fry in oil, a few at a time, at about 360°, until lightly golden. Let cool. Then frost *guantis* with a thin powdered sugar icing and decorate with colored crystals.

For colored frosting, add a drop of food coloring. Icing should be white ot pastel-colored.

MAKES 12 DOZEN

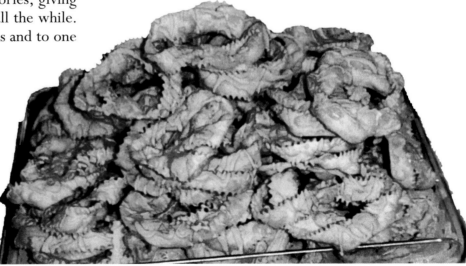

Love Knot Cookies

nodi d'amore

Love knots are always a favorite on the cookie
tables of Italian weddings.

Cookies

    1 cup butter
    1¼ cup sugar
    6 eggs
    ½ cup milk
    1 teaspoon vanilla

    ½ teaspoon salt
    4 teaspoons baking powder
    4 cups flour

Frosting

    1 lb. powdered sugar
    ½-¾ stick butter
    1-2 teaspoons milk
    1 teaspoon lemon extract

Cream butter and sugar until light. Add eggs,
milk, and vanilla. Blend dry ingredients
together and add slowly to the mix, and
continue to stir until a soft dough forms.

Drop cookies on a baking sheet a
teaspoon at a time, making sure the top
remains round. Bake at 350° for 10-12
minutes until lightly browned. Cool.

Meanwhile, mix the frosting ingredients
until they form a coating consistency. Dip
each love knot by hand into the frosting and
spread evenly over the cookie. Place cookies
on wax paper to dry.

MAKES 6 DOZEN

Italian Peach Cookies

biscotti percoca

Peach cookies are especially nice during the summer. Keep them refrigerated for a cool treat. Aunt Melina would serve them for special occasions. They are best served the same day they are made.

Aunt Melina and Uncle Paul Tursi on their wedding day

> 4 eggs
> 1 cup sugar
> 1 cup oil or 1 cup margarine, melted
> 4 teaspoons baking powder
> ¼ teaspoon salt
> 1 cup milk
> 1 shot crème de almond
> 4-5 cups flour
> 1 package pudding, cooked according to
>   package directions (We like French vanilla)
> 6 oz. package strawberry Jello

Mix eggs, sugar, salt, oil, and milk. Then add dry ingredients to make a soft dough. Roll into 3-inch balls, bake at 350° for 12 to 14 minutes, and remove from oven.

  After the balls have cooled, hollow out the bottom side of each ball with a melon baller and fill each hollow with a teaspoon of pudding. Press two balls together to make a "peach." Roll the peaches in crème de almond liqueur, then in the dry strawberry Jello powder. Pile them gently on a pretty platter.

MAKES 3 DOZEN

135

Wine Cookies

crustali

Always served at Christmas-time and at Italian weddings, these cookies melt in your mouth. They are my son Brian's favorite.

Cookies

1 cup wine
1 cup oil
6 cups or more flour
1 teaspoon baking powder
1½ teaspoons nutmeg
¾ cup sugar
2 beaten eggs
1 teaspoon vanilla
oil for frying

Frosting

1 lb. powdered sugar
½-¾ stick butter
1-2 teaspoons milk
1 teaspoon lemon extract

To make the cookies, bring the wine and oil to a boil together, then set aside to cool.

Put all dry ingredients in a large bowl. In another bowl, mix together the eggs, vanilla, sugar, and the cooled wine and oil. Add to the dry ingredients and mix well—dough should be medium soft.

Roll dough out into a long rope and cut into 1½-2 inch lengths. Roll each piece over a fork or a cut glass bowl to give it an imprint. Fry them a few at a time in hot oil (350°), and drain on paper towels. Cool.

To make the frosting, mix frosting ingredients in a large bowl until they reach a coating consistency. Add crustali and mix with hands until they are well-coated. Separate and spread out on wax paper to dry.

MAKES 6 DOZEN

Double Chocolate Biscotti

biscotti al cioccolato

Biscotti are very hard dry cookies that are meant to be dipped. This one begs to be dipped in a caffe latte or cappucino.

½ cup butter
¾ cup sugar
2 eggs
2 tablespoons Amaretto
2 cups plus 2 tablespoons flour
⅓ cup unsweetened cocoa
1½ teaspoons baking powder
¼ teaspoon salt
⅔ cup chopped almonds
⅔ cup chopped chocolate

In a mixing bowl, cream butter and sugar. Beat in eggs and Amaretto. In another bowl combine the flour, cocoa, baking powder, and salt. Add to the cream mixture and blend well. Fold in nuts and chocolate. Divide dough in half.

On a greased baking sheet, pat out dough into two logs about ½ inch high, 1½ inches wide, and 14 inches long. Bake in a 325° oven for 25 minutes. Let cool.

With a serrated knife cut 1-inch slices diagonally at a 45° angle. Place slices flat on cookie sheet and bake another 10 minutes, turning once half-way through.

Let cool and store in a covered container.

MAKES 2–3 DOZEN

Index

T

V

W

Z

About Carmela Tursi Hobbins:

Carmela is of Italian heritage with roots in Calabria in southern Italy. Her love of Italian cuisine was fostered during her childhood in Des Moines, Iowa, where her family owns a restaurant.

Inspired by her studies at La Quercia in Italy, Carmela began offering cooking classes in her own kitchen in Minneapolis, and was also the owner of the successful catering business *Occasions Catering*.

Carmela frequently travels to Italy with the sole purpose of learning new cooking methods and recipes. For further information about her classes and cooking tours please visit Carmela's web site at ***carmiescucina.com.***